50 STATES *of* CRIME

OHIO

THE CLEVELAND JOHN DOE CASE

50 STATES *of* CRIME OHIO

THE CLEVELAND JOHN DOE CASE

THIBAULT RAISSE
TRANSLATED BY LAURIE BENNETT

CRIME INK

NEW YORK

CLEVELAND JOHN DOE

Crime Ink
An Imprint of Penzler Publishers
58 Warren Street
New York, N.Y. 10007

© Editions 10/18, Département d'Univers Poche, 2023
In association with So Press/Society
English translation copyright: © 2025 by Laurie Bennett

First Crime Ink edition

Cover design by Charles Perry, inspired by the French language
edition cover design by Nicolas Caminade

Interior design by Maria Fernandez

Library of Congress Control Number: 2024918141

Paperback ISBN: 978-1-61316-633-8
eBook ISBN: 978-1-61316-634-5

10 9 8 7 6 5 4 3 2 1

Printed in the United States of America
Distributed by W. W. Norton & Company

Contents

"He was odd. And odd sometimes meant dangerous."

—James Renner,
The Man from Primrose Lane

PART 1
LIVE ONCE, DIE TWICE

Chapter 1

When a day of investigations ended with anything but a stop at Demarco's, it was kind of a bust. An ad boasted "Best donuts in Eastlake." In the town of eighteen thousand, where the coffee shop on Lakeshore Boulevard had only one competitor, the claim was a relatively safe bet. But anyway, if Detective Chris Bowersock had made this place his regular spot, it wasn't so much for the quality of the menu as for its proximity to the police station, just across the street.

Bowersock had already stopped by that morning, in plain clothes, en route to the home of a heroin dealer he'd been staking out for weeks. The server had automatically brought him his usual: one coffee, double cream, no sugar. Now, like at the end of every shift, Bowersock stood at the counter before heading to the office one last time to tackle the day's paperwork.

"Double cream," said the server as she handed him an oversized cup.

Bowersock had just picked up his drink when the radio wrapped around his left wrist crackled. The 9-1-1 dispatcher's voice sounded scratchy over the static. "Body found at the Dover Place Apartments."

Well shit. When a body turned up near the end of a shift, even if it was just an elderly guy who had died of natural causes, it always meant he'd get home late.

Bowersock checked his watch—3:34 P.M.

Strange time to die.

Born and raised in Eastlake, Bowersock didn't need to pull out a map. He'd known the town like the back of his hand well before joining law enforcement. The rental units were just eight blocks west on Lakeshore Boulevard, the main artery running along Lake Erie and connecting all the neighborhoods in the small town in Cleveland's northern suburbs. A roadside sign that read "Dover Place Apartments" had been staked into the lawn, marking the entrance.

With two hundred twenty-nine prefab units, Dover Place looked like a high-end trailer park. Advertisements published in the *News-Herald*, Lake County's daily paper, described "beautiful studio, one-bedroom, and two-bedroom apartments surrounded by green space." The brochure boasted nearby lake access, just a half mile away, the joy of communal living, on-site maintenance services, and, for those excluded from the suburban elite, the unique privilege afforded by single-story housing: the American dream of sitting in a rocking chair on the patio and drinking a Bud while ribs sizzle on the grill.

Bowersock pulled into a random spot in the vast Dover Place parking lot. There was no point in trying to park in the shade; a few elms nearby cast a paltry shadow, providing little shelter from the oppressive heat. It was July 30, 2002, and the thermometer read 95°F. For the Midwest, this was unusually warm, even at this time of year, and the scorching temperatures had held every day for the past month. Between calls to challenge Saddam Hussein and invade Iraq on the eve of the first anniversary of 9/11, the *News-Herald* had already predicted that if the heatwave persisted into August, the summer of 2002 would be the hottest on record for northern Ohio.

A slender man in his thirties came to meet Bowersock. He wore gray work pants with his name and position embroidered onto a white polo shirt: "Jeffrey Offak—Service Manager." For all repairs, from leaky faucets and broken AC units to hot water that wasn't quite hot enough, Jeffrey Offak was the Dover Place handyman. He confirmed that he'd been the one to make the 9-1-1 call.

The apartment C tenant, a house painter and ex-convict, had phoned Offak's office earlier that day to report he hadn't seen his studio D neighbor for three or four days. *Huh, I haven't either,* thought Offak, who usually crossed paths with the retiree every day while he was out on his daily walk around the property. So, Offak knocked on his door—no answer. He used his spare key to get inside, where he discovered Joseph Chandler's lifeless body within seconds.

As they walked the couple hundred yards toward unit D and the body, Bowersock questioned Offak with thinly veiled criticism. What made him think he had the right to enter the premises before the police?

"It's my job," said Offak.

"But it's a potential crime scene."

"How would you have known if I hadn't gone inside?"

Bowersock let it go.

Apartment D was a typical Dover studio, and for good reason; every unit on the premises had been assembled in a factory, according to a standardized process, then transported here by convoy. Every apartment consisted of 260-square-foot modules: one for each studio, two joined together for one-bedroom units, and three for the two-bedroom apartments. From outside, Bowersock noticed the blinds were closed in both large windows overlooking the patio. Offak warned him that the AC had been switched off and the heat in the unit was unbearable. As for the smell, he added, it was so foul that after leaving the apartment, he'd suddenly been struck by a wave of nausea and dry-heaved on the lawn.

Bowersock was no stranger to the smell of a decaying body, something akin to spoiled red meat. And while he didn't love it, he found it tolerable. In his eight years of service with the Eastlake crime unit, he'd seen his fair share of decomposing cadavers. Admittedly, Eastlake only got to investigate about one homicide per year, while Cleveland, just twenty miles south, would rack up an average of one hundred in the same time span. But local detectives here were accustomed to DOAs, people found dead on arrival, and were called to respond to them at least once a month. Working-class towns, even the ones in relatively good economic shape, like Eastlake, were not spared the scourge of loneliness and the many suicides and natural deaths that went unnoticed by relatives or neighbors for weeks on end.

Without waiting for backup, Bowersock stepped onto the porch of the studio apartment and asked to be let in. Offak complied, first opening the screen door. Behind it, the front door was shut. The detective frowned. It was covered in flies.

Bad sign, he thought as Offak unlocked the unit.

The moment he set foot in the apartment, Bowersock fell to his knees.

When the door opened, it unleashed a wall of blistering hot air mixed with a putrid stench, like a boiler flashback from an abandoned slaughterhouse. His breath caught in his throat as he recoiled and quickly took in the scene. The old sepia wallpaper was teeming with flies in a chaotic, buzzing cloud. He held the radio up to his mouth and could already taste the decay. "It's Bowersock. I'm at the Dover DOA. Call in the fire department, we need respirators."

A few minutes later, the firefighters pulled in at the same time as Bowersock's partner, Ted Kroczak. Both men had grown up in Eastlake, within a few blocks of each other, and had gone to the same schools. As kids, they used to hang out after school on the sandy Will-O-Way Beach by the lake just down the road. In winter, hidden under a white sheet, they would meet in front of the library and throw snowballs at a patrol officer's cruiser. Fifteen years later, when they joined the force, that same cop, the one who used to chase after them, became their mentor.

You could write a police comedy based on this ride-or-die pair. Their fellow officers called them "Starsky and Hutch," but they saw themselves more as Riggs and Murtaugh from *Lethal Weapon*. Bowersock, aged thirty-two, was the Riggs in this pair. A man with a short fuse who relied on instincts to make judgments and take action, he could explode over a simple misunderstanding. At thirty-six, Kroczak had a short crew cut and was built like a quarterback. He was the quiet partner, the coolheaded mastermind. If the Eastlake police force had an outstanding reputation throughout the county, they owed much of it to the duo's outright daring work.

After the morning briefing, rather than wait for cases to come in, Bowersock and Kroczak would set off to infiltrate a biker gang or a drug ring. In the evening, once the stress of the assignment had subsided, they would run through a play-by-play of the day's tense moments over a beer.

Both men swore they would take a bullet to save their partner. Kroczak almost made good on his promise the day he threw himself at a cocaine dealer who had managed to grab Bowersock's assault rifle. Like all true brothers-in-arms, they once fought each other in a bar on a drunken night. To this day, neither one remembers what started it, but Kroczak was the first to throw a punch. As chairs sailed through the air, a bartender yelled, "Call the cops!" to which his jaded boss answered, "They are the cops."

Bowersock and Kroczak first slipped into white Tyvek suits, then each strapped on a Scott Air-Pak, a backpack fitted with a small oxygen bottle, typically used by firefighters to prevent asphyxiation. They set a large fan on the doormat and pointed it outside to clear out the stale air in the apartment. With Kroczak in step, Bowersock entered the unit. Geared up and swarmed by flies, they looked like beekeepers exploring a giant hive.

The apartment featured brown carpeting and dark wood furniture with beige paneling, which lent the space the yellowish hue of a used cigarette filter. To the right of the entrance was an open Murphy bed. A gray sofa with a square pattern was set against the left-hand wall. Above it hung a framed photo of a Gothic castle on a hilltop in Spain, which was later identified as the Alcázar of Segovia.

The TV, pressed up against the right-hand armrest, faced away from the front door. To the right of the sofa, in line with the bed, stood a closet and a tall shelf, both practically empty. In the first hung a single gray jacket and one red tie. On the shelf were four folded short-sleeve shirts, one white analog clock radio, one pair of Nike shoes in the box, and one portable safe. The minimalism and outdated look of the place added to the feeling that they were inspecting a motel room in a David Lynch film.

At the left end of the apartment, before the kitchenette, a desk drew their attention. Near an antiquated PC with a 3.5-inch floppy disk drive, a rectangular mouse, and a faded keyboard, two books were stacked on top of each other: *Making Money with Your Computer at Home* and *How to Make Money in Stocks*, a best-selling book by millionaire investor William O'Neil. But Bowersock and Kroczak were most interested in two objects to the left of the computer: one clear ziplock bag containing what looked like roughly fifteen loose bullets, which they recognized as .38 caliber, and one gun case lined with gray foam. The case was open, the weapon missing.

A calendar featuring large squares was open to the month of June and partially hidden by the case. A magnifying glass, eyeglasses, and an analog watch had been left on the calendar and contrasted with the general atmosphere of the inert space that seemed frozen in time. It was as though that little desk space had been both the only witness to the recent existence of an occupant and the epicenter of his last moments of life.

Both detectives stared at it for a moment, noticing that the days of the month had been crossed out up to and including July 24. Six days ago.

This left only the bathroom. It was behind the large closet and accessed through a nook in the kitchenette. Hampered by their airtight suits, Bowersock and Kroczak slowly crept toward the bathroom, every movement causing them to sweat profusely. This might be a crime scene, so it had to be preserved as much as possible until the arrival of forensic technician Louis Formick.

Bowersock was the first to peer into the bathroom. The door had been left open. As he glimpsed the body splayed out on the carpet, face down, he felt dread in the pit of his stomach. He had never seen a body in such an advanced state of decomposition, and—to his horror—he was sure he'd seen it move. But that was impossible. Nothing could be more dead than this poor man. Yet he had no doubt he'd seen something that looked alive in this mass of putrefying flesh. With one more look at the body, he realized he wasn't crazy. The back of Joseph Chandler's skull teemed with hundreds of maggots.

His body lay across the room, on his right side and in the fetal position, with his head turned toward the bathtub and feet by the sink. His skin was blistered and speckled with brown spots, like a potato left in the oven for too long. He wore a white shirt with gray stripes tucked into navy-blue chinos. The body was steeping in a pool of sticky black liquid, a mixture of all the gases and bodily fluids released in the decomposition process. A scorching summer, closed windows, and the air-conditioning being shut off were prime conditions for accelerated decay. Bowersock and Kroczak realized they'd arrived at the worst possible time. Two days earlier, the state of decomposition would have been more tolerable; two days later, mummification would have begun, drying out the tissue and shutting down the buffet for all these maggots.

What little blood spatter there was, was around the sink. One small spot near the drain, a few drops on the faux marble edge. Nothing on the mirror above the sink, nor the walls or ceiling. In the bathtub, they found one .38-gauge bullet casing. As Bowersock stepped closer to the body, he spotted the tip of a black metal tube under the man's chest, on the left side. It was the barrel of a revolver.

When he'd heard the dispatcher's call on the radio, Bowersock had initially assumed they would be dealing with an old man who had been done in by the heat wave. In the end, the reality was much more visually striking but not all that much more spectacular. The front door had been locked from the inside, there were no signs of a break-in, the body position with the revolver under the torso was that of a person who had fallen forward, and there were only minute traces of blood, only one spent bullet casing, and maggots at the back of the skull swarming in what looked like a cavity. All evidence pointed to the same conclusion: The man had put a gun in his mouth and shot himself in the head.

Formick, the forensic technician, stepped into the apartment with a camera around his neck and began capturing the scene. He, too, had no doubt that this was a suicide, but every death had to be handled as a homicide until the Cleveland medical examiner could rule out foul play. Formick took a moment to bag some evidence: the revolver, of course, the minisafe, the two books conspicuously left by the computer, as well as a wallet and a set of seven keys found in the dead man's chinos. He figured there might be a suicide note, an explanation, either in the safe or slipped between the pages of a book.

Finally, they were allowed to move the body. Bowersock and Kroczak each grabbed an arm, while Lou picked up the feet. As soon as the torso left the ground, a cracking sound made them all jump. Kroczak looked over at a dazed Bowersock, who was left holding an arm that had been pulled from its socket like a chicken wing. The detectives were complementary partners both in the field and in their dark sense of humor, which they used as an outlet. Kroczak was the first to crack a joke. "Put it back!"

Once the coroner's assistant arrived, operations came to an end. After a visual examination, he confirmed the police's suicide-by-gunshot hypothesis. The stench was so unbearable they had to double bag the body. Bowersock and Kroczak gave up on trying to get fingerprints off the deceased. While bagging the body, the skin of the arms had slid right off. Like a soft prawn pulled from its tail, bones and muscles were left exposed, rendering any further attempts futile. The face, consumed by maggots, had become nothing more than a hole. But Offak, the service manager, described a fairly small man in his sixties with an average build, and this body appeared to fit the description.

Vita Ebbert, the Dover Place manager, brought her tenant's records to the detectives. This included his lease, renewed in March, along with emergency contacts and the registration form he had filled out on his first day in the apartment. In the Dover Place Apartments, where rent was expensive and all units were furnished, tenant turnover rates were high. Most renters were in a transitional phase—people going through a divorce, employees in between jobs, folks waiting to buy a house in the area—and tended to land there for just a couple of months. In the studio apartments, which were not equipped with washing machines and where only single occupancy was allowed, turnover rates were even higher.

Joseph Chandler, aged sixty-four, had lived in his apartment for seventeen years.

A specialized van brought the body to Dr. Rizzo, the Lake County coroner who was responsible for all of the county's criminal cases. He would first conduct an external examination and then, if he had any doubts as to the cause of death, an autopsy.

Bowersock and Kroczak walked back to their vehicles. As they'd feared, the VapoRub they'd smeared under their noses did nothing to repel the lingering smell of death.

"The only weird part of this story is the way this guy lived," mused Bowersock.

"The cupboards are almost empty, even though he'd been there for years," Kroczak added. "Did you see the books on the desk?"

"Yeah, and besides, why would you try to get rich if you'd already decided to off yourself?"

"Maybe he was broke. It's a good motive for suicide."

They split up for the day. Kroczak went home to his fiancée, while Bowersock made his way to the police station. As the first responder, it would be his job to write a report about the body discovery. He drafted a precise account of his findings and delivered his provisional conclusion: suicide by firearm.

When Bowersock had initially found the body prone in the bathroom, he'd been struck by one tiny detail. He hadn't mentioned it to his partner and didn't think it was worth including in the report either. It was a simple deduction, quite disturbing but not all that relevant to the investigation. It came to him when his mind connected two observations: the body position on the carpet and the drops of blood in the sink.

As Bowersock connected the dots, the seconds leading up to the killing came to him in a flash.

When he'd pressed the trigger, Joseph Chandler had been staring at himself in the mirror.

Chapter 2

A teacher once asked eight-year-old Tom Doyle what he wanted to be when he grew up, and the boy blurted out, "A hobo!" Unimpressed, the teacher told him to think of a vocation more honorable than the life of a homeless vagabond. *What a strange reprimand,* thought the child. What could possibly be more enviable than a life of adventure with a bag slung over your shoulder, hopping onto the first train that passes by without even knowing where you are headed or what tomorrow will bring? To be left in peace, Tom redacted and said, "A teacher, like my father." But he didn't believe that for one second. Neither could this son of blue-collar Marxist obedience, imagine he would eventually don a police uniform every day for nearly forty years.

For generations, the Doyle family had relied on Pennsylvania coal to put food on the table. The town of eight hundred people where Tom had grown up in the 1950s, just south of Pittsburgh, was also the home of the Coal Queen Pageant, a pageant organized by the industry union to crown the most beautiful worker or worker's wife.

As a young boy, Tom lived with his parents and ten siblings in a red-brick neighborhood built for mine workers. While his grandfather and uncle were still pushing wagons, his father decided to break with the family line, choosing instead to become a teacher. In the evenings, he would come home with clean nails, but his modest pay would dry up over the summer break. Thus, every summer, he resigned himself to laboring in an automotive parts factory across the Ohio state line in the bustling metropolis of Cleveland. In 1961, he moved there with his wife and gaggle of children.

At the time, Cleveland was the Silicon Valley of steel. The steel industry, which was already flourishing at the beginning of the twentieth century, exploded during the Second World War due to demand for weapons and military vehicles. A modern-day Eldorado, the Midwest had built most of the country's metallurgical plants around the five Great Lakes. Every year, these American steel towns drew in tens of thousands of workers from the South who brought their rural ways and Southern speak to a land that had historically been occupied by progressive, refined German immigrants.

At the turn of 1950, "The Cleve" was ranked the sixth most populous city in the United States with nearly a million residents, ahead of Boston, Detroit, and Baltimore. Perpetually surpassed by its sister city, Chicago, Cleveland quite naturally borrowed the town's monumental neoclassical architecture from its Lake Michigan rival. The Terminal Tower, designed to look like the Empire State Building, even held the title of "tallest skyscraper in the United States," after New York City.

In the early 1960s, the Doyle family's move to Cleveland coincided with the beginning of the city's slow decline. Steel mills were moving to the Pacific Coast to reduce transportation and export costs before simply relocating to Asia. With the development of urban highways and interstates, the upper and middle classes fled air that had been rendered unbreathable by blast furnaces to settle down in greener neighborhoods in the suburbs.

In 1965, the "Sixth City" fell to twelfth place among the country's largest cities. Around the same time, the first race riots in the civil rights movement were breaking out. Tensions would remain high until 1968, after the election of Carl Stokes, the first African American mayor of a major city in all of the United States.

On the morning of June 22, 1969, residents thought they might be hallucinating and called the fire department. The Cuyahoga River was on fire. The river, which snaked between buildings and fed into Lake Erie, had become so saturated with toxic chemicals that people would sometimes witness bubbling at the surface, slow and thick, like a potion in a cartoon. The national media flocked to the tragedy, portraying it as a symbol of the city's recent downturn. As unemployment and insecurity grew, urban flight soon spread to the working classes, leaving downtown Cleveland to the poor and the marginalized.

The Doyles lived in a house outside the downtown core and, anyway, they didn't have time to stray far from the steel mill that employed Tom's father. Every day, he would work a night shift at the factory, get a few hours of sleep, and then show up for work as a teacher in neighboring Eastlake, Lake County. It was the price to pay to feed eleven mouths.

Located twenty miles north of Cleveland along Lake Erie, Lake County—like the rest of Ohio—was a little bellwether for American elections. The local ballot count had systematically predicted national results to come, whether in favor of Republicans or Democrats, which locals alternately supported, according to the latest polls. Halfway between the ghettoized neighborhoods of East Cleveland and the two-million-dollar mansions of Chagrin Falls, the average annual salary was quite similar to the national average.

In Lake County, moderation was more than just a statistical truth; residents had made it a way of life. Responsibly mowed lawns vastly outnumbered properties with political or vindictive yard signs. People drove just over the speed limit so they would appear neither too disciplined nor lawless. Motorists were happy to fasten their seat belts, while motorcyclists could ride without a helmet. Every resident was armed, but no one pulled their weapons out of the locked cabinets in which they gathered dust. Lake County was a kind of Middle America, or Middle-Earth, invisible to news and pop culture radars, too poor to inspire dreams but not poor enough to be pitied. This was middle-class America, watching TV in slippers, peaceful, pragmatic, and conformist, not out of a desire to follow but as a matter of principle.

Tom Doyle earned his bachelor's degree in 1981. His interest in science and the region's industrial impact led him to study chemistry in college, although he had no particular career in mind. When he got married and had a son in the same year, Doyle had to come up with a more concrete plan. He started to look for a little work, first part-time, then full-time.

Meanwhile, local police departments were constantly recruiting personnel. In Cleveland, this was the result of police brutality cases that had depleted the force while neighboring communities were calling for more feet on the ground to tackle rising crime rates. His left-wing education had made him wary of uniforms in general, especially those worn by cops, whom he considered to be abusing an excessive degree of power. In the end, his sense of paternal duty overcame his reluctance.

After passing a written exam, Tom Doyle joined the police academy like a prisoner of war forced to serve the enemy. In training, he openly criticized the institution, for which he was mocked by his peers and some higher-ups. Still, it didn't stop him from being recruited by the Eastlake police. *I'll stay here for seven or eight months, set aside some money, and then go back to college,* he convinced himself. But the unthinkable ensued. Doyle realized that being in a position of authority was a guilty pleasure. He immediately booked an appointment with a psychiatrist to treat what he deemed a sadistic inclination. "You're not doing anything wrong. On the contrary, you're serving society," explained a bemused specialist.

You can't argue with science.

At the time, the Eastlake police station employed thirteen officers, all rank-and-file patrolmen. There was no point in opening a criminal investigation unit because crimes like murders and rapes, and even more common crimes like robberies and drug trafficking, were extremely rare. Summers brought about an uptick in activity. Young people drinking on Will-O-Way Beach ended up sick or involved in fights, and pleasure boats collided on days when the swell was especially powerful. The rest of the time, regular days came with their share of road accidents, exhibitionists, and packs of beer stolen from gas stations. Reporters at the *News-Herald* had to dig through Cleveland's criminal history to fill the pages of the local paper. And when a homicide disrupted this routine, it was always a family tragedy that could be solved within a day—that is, when the culprit didn't turn himself in first.

Doyle immediately felt at home, and he already had the portly build of a jolly, donut-loving cop. Still, he would have welcomed a little more action or, at the very least, a case that would allow him to test his investigative prowess. His wish was granted one morning in 1985 when waves lapping at the shores of Lake Erie delivered the body of a decapitated woman. A patrol officer had to be pulled off the street to handle the case full-time, so Doyle volunteered to take it on.

He identified the victim, an Eastlake resident, and then found out that her husband had disappeared after the crime was committed. The guy was a disciple of Hare Krishna. Doyle called and wrote to all of the Krishna temples in the United States and beyond to expose the husband in case he sought asylum with his brethren. His calls and letters began with an appeal for help. "I don't want to tarnish your religion. I respect it. I just want this guy to be tried for what he did."

Krishna followers cooperated and reported that the suspect was in Cleveland, then Texas, England, Belgium, Greece, France, and finally New York. The man was eventually arrested while attempting to cross the Canadian border. The FBI and its limitless resources could not have done any better than Tom Doyle armed with a landline and a pencil. "I'm not a smart guy, but I don't give up," he explained. The head of the Eastlake Police Department agreed and launched a crime unit within the department, with Doyle as the lead investigator.

❖

Seventeen years later, four detectives were working under Lieutenant Doyle's command, including Bowersock and Kroczak, his "best guys." They got along so well that hierarchical barriers were quickly broken down, and Doyle had a standing invitation to join his men at the bar in the evenings. It was during one of these nights out that he earned the nickname "Cheeks." When a patron threw fries at him for no apparent reason, a tipsy Doyle pulled out his service weapon and demanded a little respect. Then he slid the gun into the back of his pants, sat down, and accidentally triggered a shot that grazed his rear—his "cheek."

Around the time Joseph Chandler's body was found in the Dover Place Apartments, the Eastlake crime unit was working undercover with FBI support to take down an extensive illegal gambling ring that had proliferated throughout northern Ohio. Against this busy backdrop, it would have been difficult for the case of the studio D body to mobilize authorities. In fact, it wasn't even a case. With a simple visual examination and a phone call, the Cleveland coroner had declared the death a suicide by firearm. Sad as it may be, blowing one's brains out was still legal. Violent deaths were of interest to the police only in the absence of consent.

Still, to appease his conscience, Bowersock ran the elderly man's name through the system. He found his full name, Joseph Newton Chandler III, and the information on his driver's license: born March 11, 1937, in Buffalo, New York, five feet seven, 160 pounds, brown hair, gray eyes. His estimates based on the body—age, height, weight—all lined up.

Then there was the photo from his driver's license, which had been provided by the applicant in 1999 at the age of sixty-two. It showed a wrinkled and impassive face, with short, fine white hair running from one ear to the other like a headband, a snub nose, thin lips, oversized eyeglasses that looked like safety goggles, a gray jacket over a white shirt, and a navy-blue tie. He was an average guy in every way, except for his strange, ambiguous stare, something between surprise and anxious anticipation.

Before closing the case, the police still had to notify the poor man's family, one final formality. Two names were listed on the emergency contact form Joseph Chandler had filled out. There was Vita Ebbert, the property manager, who was surprised to find this out since she knew nothing about her tenant's personal life. And there was a couple, Mike and Marilyn Onderisin. Chandler had included their address and landline and listed them as "friends." Bowersock dialed the number and shared the sad news over voicemail. The next day, Mike Onderisin called back and apologized, explaining that he and his wife had been on vacation in Cape May, New Jersey's famous seaside resort. They were now available to speak with investigators.

On August 2, the Onderisins made their way to the Eastlake police station. The offices were at a busy intersection across the street from a skate park, by the town hall and the fire station. A soda dispenser in the reception area provided a little comfort for visitors as they waited to be led into the offices through the building's double doors. Still in shock over the news about the man they called "Joe," the Onderisins walked along a thick gray carpet to Tom Doyle's desk, where he invited them to sit down. Bowersock was also present.

From the very first questions, what was supposed to be a routine deposition became more of an interrogation. Even though he was sure this had been a suicide, Lieutenant Doyle could not help but take on the dry and cold tone of a man who would not be lied to. He knew it was a bad habit, especially when speaking with bereaved relatives, but he couldn't help himself. His default was to address each witness as a person of interest, as someone who, though not a suspect at that particular moment, might become one sooner or later. The Onderisins did not grasp this nuance. What exactly were they accused of doing? Bowersock was hardly more agreeable. Before their arrival, he had run their names through the system, just in case.

The Onderisins kept this unpleasant impression to themselves and gave their deposition. Mike, aged sixty-one, had met Joseph Chandler in 1985 at Lubrizol in Painesville, Lake County. The company was an American chemical giant, and this location manufactured lubricated oils and products for industrial use. Both men worked in the electrical design department, where they were office neighbors. Their team designed electrical schematics. Chandler was a tinkering genius who could fix any breakdown anywhere in the factory, regardless of its nature.

As a colleague, he was quiet to the extreme, shy, and highly solitary. Mike, who described himself as quite the opposite—nothing brought him more joy than going to a baseball game with a group of friends—felt bad for the guy. To call their relationship "friendly" would be an exaggeration, but they were a little more than colleagues. In seventeen years, the Onderisins had invited Joseph Chandler to their home twice: once for dinner and once for a birthday party.

Since Chandler's retirement in 1997, Mike Onderisin had called him at least once a year.

While Lieutenant Doyle did care about these details, he was most interested in identifying the next of kin who would take care of the funeral and the estate. On this point, the Onderisin spouses were of little use. As far as they knew, Joseph Chandler had no wife and no children. He had once told them that he'd been married to a Cuban woman in Florida, where he lived when he was younger. He claimed that before that, he had grown up in East Liverpool, 110 miles south of Eastlake, near the Pennsylvania border. That's all they knew about his past. "Joe" was no more chatty about this aspect of his life than any other.

Without a will or known heirs, the law stipulated that the estate of the deceased would revert to the state. But Joseph Chandler was not as poor as his frugal home and reading material had initially suggested. One of the keys found in his pants was for a vehicle parked in front of the apartment, a 1988 General Motors pickup truck. It was in good condition, worth about $1,000. But the real surprise came from the request for bank statements. Chandler's four accounts at Bank One held a total balance of $58,000. The man wasn't exactly broke, as detectives had initially assumed.

Doyle explained to the Onderisins that there was one way to keep the money from ending up in state coffers. A colleague or friend who was close enough to Chandler, or simply concerned about his memory, could launch a search for his next of kin. Mike would have to apply to the probate court, the estate court, which would then appoint him as the administrator of the estate. The accounts of the deceased would be used to cover expenses related to his search under the supervision of the court. If the estate administrator managed to find a next of kin, this person would pocket the remainder. If he failed, the remaining money would be turned over to state coffers.

The Onderisins were not sure they wanted to take on such responsibility but promised to think it over.

On August 30, a funeral was held in Joseph Chandler's memory at the crematorium in Mentor, Ohio. Aside from the pastor, only Mike and Marilyn Onderisin, who had paid the $1,600 in fees, were present. The urn was then stored in the Painesville cemetery columbarium under a gentle sun.

On September 13, Mike Onderisin filed an application with the probate court, and it was accepted.

To move forward, he secured the services of lawyer James O'Leary, an acquaintance of his wife. O'Leary had been a licensed member of the Ohio State Bar Association for six years, and while he specialized in wealth management, the search for next of kin was not his specialty per se. He began by publishing notices in the *News-Herald* classified section and made an advance payment for three publications.

"To the unknown heirs and legatees of Joseph N. Chandler, deceased. You are hereby notified that the decedent died on July 24, 2002. Mike J. Onderisin has filed an application in this court asking to be appointed to administer the decedent's estate. If you wish to be considered for appointment to do so, you must apply to this Court."

The announcement first appeared in an issue published on October 30, 2002. The text was listed under an advertisement promoting the launch of an innovative service to sell used cars "over the Internet" and after an article about the democratization of DVDs, which had been so successful that they would soon render VHS tapes obsolete.

As he waited for an heir to come forward, O'Leary contacted local managers at Lubrizol, Chandler's last employer. He didn't learn anything useful except that the deceased had $16,000 in an employee savings plan he had signed in 1996. This brought the total wealth

of the deceased up to $75,000. The savings plan state-
ment came with another surprise: Chandler had desig-
nated the Red Cross as the sole beneficiary of his plan.
O'Leary notified the court and, on behalf of his client,
made arrangements to have the funds transferred to the
organization.

Nothing came of the ads published in the local paper.
No heirs had fallen from the sky, so they would need
to be sought out. O'Leary then enlisted the services of
Mike Lewis, a thirty-five-year-old private investigator
whose dream of becoming a police officer had been
thwarted by a youth spent on the wrong side of the law.
Lewis had been the manager of a pizzeria for thirteen
years before making a late-game career change. And
although he didn't wear the uniform, at least he could
run investigations.

In a strange coincidence, Lewis had lived at the
Dover Place Apartments when he was about eighteen.
He started by interviewing Mike Onderisin over the
phone, hoping to find an obscure, loose thread he might
pull to unravel the mystery. But it was to no avail. He
then turned to an online database for licensed detectives
that listed all public records for the two hundred ninety
million Americans living throughout the fifty states. It
worked like a search engine. The user entered the last

name, first name, and date of birth of an individual, and then the tool would spit out all information collected by the government (address, criminal record, military service, banking issues, etc.). Apart from his marital status and the Eastlake address, Joseph Chandler's page was empty.

Lewis then examined the documents provided by O'Leary, those collected by the police at the Dover Place apartment. Among these files, he found the list of emergency contacts that included the Onderisins' phone number and the registration form Chandler had filled out upon his arrival at the Dover Place Apartments in October 1985. In his characteristic slanted capital letters, Chandler had also listed the name and address of a sister: Mary R. Wilson, 1823 Center Street, in Columbus, the capital of Ohio. In a box labeled "Phone number," he had scribbled "None." Lewis immediately searched his database, but there was no woman with that name in Columbus or the surrounding area. Even more surprising was the fact that this address was fictitious. There was no 1823 Center Street in Columbus, Ohio.

Lewis wanted to see this with his own eyes. Maybe there was an error in the database, and, after all, Columbus was only a three-hour drive from Lake County. On location, he did find a Center Street, but the last home displayed street number 1124. With a photo of Joseph's driver's license in hand, Lewis went around the neighborhood hoping to stir up memories. The locals didn't recognize Mary R. Wilson's name, and no one had ever seen the man hanging around the neighborhood.

When he had taken on the case, Lewis figured a half-day's work would be enough to close it. Now, the $1,800 he'd quoted felt like a meager payment for his time. Back at his office, he took a new approach to the case. With one phone call to the Buffalo Office of the city clerk, he was able to obtain a copy of Chandler's birth certificate, which was publicly available. Joseph was the son of Ellen Chandler née Kaaber, born in Morton, Pennsylvania, and Joseph Newton Chandler II, born in Weatherford, Texas.

With his database, Lewis retrieved a list of all Chandlers in and around Weatherford and then called them, one by one, hoping to come across a family member. One man, fifty-year-old Danny Chandler, stood out because of his strange behavior. He claimed to have no relationship with Joseph Chandler and then suddenly hung up. Lewis had been able to leave him his number, and Danny called back a month later. Through a genealogy search, the man had identified a Joseph Newton Chandler II on his father's side. Although he had never heard of this man from Eastlake who had committed suicide, he could be a cousin. When Lewis explained that the goal of his investigation was to appoint an heir, Danny insinuated that he knew what this was about and then hung up again and stopped answering his calls.

On April 15, 2003, after five months of work, Lewis handed his report over to O'Leary. In the document, he recounted his curious conversations with Danny Chandler and shared his certainty that the man was connected to the Chandler from the Dover Place Apartments, although he had no proof. Lewis concluded his report with the suggestion that, though he had failed in his mission, a four-hundred-dollar increase for his time and effort would be justified.

What he did not know was that, at the same time, another private detective had been quietly tasked with the case and had solved the puzzle. And, in doing so, he had opened up the most unlikely case of his career.

Chapter 3

Larry Morrow should never have stuck his nose in the Chandler case. A simple private investigator, he was technically barred from participating in any legal search for heirs. Only licensed lawyers were eligible to be appointed by judges in the probate court to assist the public administrator—Mike Onderisin, in this case—in his search. While it wasn't technically illegal, Judge Ted Klammer had shown some flexibility with his own rules when he reached out to Morrow by phone in the fall of 2002. "We just got this case, and I think you should take a look at it," he casually suggested.

Klammer and the private investigator were no strangers. They were childhood friends, and fifty-eight-year-old Morrow was considered one of the most experienced and respected finders of missing heirs in all of the United States. With a thick mustache and hungry eyes reminiscent of a young Burt Reynolds, he had, if not invented the craft, at the very least, perfected the business as no one had before. The concept was like child's play. When the holder of a bank account died without any known family, Morrow would track down an heir and give them access to the payload, less his 30 percent commission.

Apart from the search itself, the main difficulty in this exercise was to legally seal the deal in a country where money is more sacred than the dead. Morrow hailed from a family of assembly line workers and had dropped out of high school. He had spent two years refining the perfect contract before pocketing his first payment.

For more than thirty years, Morrow had started every day early in the morning going over the latest legal notices in the newspaper. He would read about cases of estates with no heirs that had just been opened at the Painesville courthouse and then make his way there to dig into those with the most generous funds. His investigations took him to all fifty states, Germany, England, and France. He could spend hours walking through deserted cemeteries in search of a date of death or a maiden name needed to fill in parts of a family tree.

His best commissions had exceeded $100,000. At the height of his glory days in the 1980s, he had four employees working in a two-floor office and traveled by private jet. Then the competition became increasingly stiff. But Morrow had lost none of his know-how nor the joy he felt every time he tackled an unsolved mystery.

When he hung up after his conversation with Judge Klammer, Morrow rushed over to the courthouse to read the documents. The case consisted of a three-page form Mike Onderisin had filled out, a request to be appointed as the administrator of the estate of the late Joseph Chandler. The form indicated that there were "no heirs" and listed the civil status of the deceased, which he made sure to take note of. But only one piece of information really caught his attention: The total value of the estate was close to $80,000. Not a bad deal.

Morrow followed his usual routine. First, he looked through the county's civil status records. They delivered nothing useful about this Chandler, nor did they reveal the existence of another person with the same last name. Then, just as Mike Lewis was doing at the same time, a few miles away, he asked for and obtained the birth certificate of the deceased. But unlike his colleague, Morrow decided to look into Chandler's mother in an attempt to locate family members. It was a matter of probability.

Kaaber, her maiden name, was uncommon, and this limited the likelihood of coming across people with the same name who had no ties to the deceased. His professional database scanned all fifty states and provided a first match: an elderly woman named Kaaber, born in New York State, like Joseph Chandler. She was now living across the country, in Riverside County, in the suburbs of Los Angeles. To follow the lead more quickly, Morrow reached out to Dave Franklin, an old associate on the West Coast.

Both were heir hunters, and they had known each other for twenty years. In LA, Franklin's name was an institution in the industry. He looked like Will Ferrell's doppelgänger. Once, a Hollywood producer had even contacted him for a film project loosely based on his peculiar profession. Franklin had agreed to read the script and consult on its credibility, for which he earned the title of "technical advisor" once production began. The result was a comedy called *Nickel and Dime* that was released in 1992, decimated by critics, and shown in theaters for all of forty-eight hours. In the room where Franklin had come to witness the carnage with his own eyes, only one other audience member had made the trip.

When the lights came back on, Franklin couldn't resist the urge to ask why the guy was there. "Is your name also in the credits?"

Franklin had figured out, probably better than any of his colleagues, how to approach a potential heir. First, never tell them you are a private investigator—it makes people tense up. The best approach is to say nothing at all, or if there's too much pressure, present yourself as an "investigator specializing in estates." In fact, when naming his business, Franklin opted for the deliberately nebulous "Equity Title Search" and soon removed the magnifying glass that had been featured on his first business cards.

Second, it's best to establish first contact over the phone to make sure the target has not already been scooped up by a speedier colleague and to avoid unnecessary travel in such cases.

Lastly, ask questions that are as open-ended as possible. The goal is to let the person explore their family tree and connect the dots on their own, which will then lead them to either identify the deceased or confirm the absence of family ties without forcing you to show your hand.

The phone call made to Ms. Kaaber was no exception to this tried-and-tested process. Franklin called from his office, an annex built in his backyard, in the historic Hancock Park neighborhood. As he picked up the receiver, he looked over the information Morrow had passed along. The lead seemed solid. It would take just a minute or two.

"Hello?"

"Hello, ma'am, my name is Dave Franklin, and I'm looking for members of the Kaaber family."

"Yes, that's my name."

He could tell from her tone that she was curious. The hardest part was over. Franklin asked her to describe her family tree and interrupted at the first mention of Ellen's name.

"Who was this Ellen?"

"My aunt."

"Was she married?"

"Yes, to Joseph Newton Chandler II. They had a son with the same name, Joseph Newton Chandler III."

"So, this child is your cousin?"

"*Was.*"

Shit. She already knew. So much for his commission.

"So you're aware of his suicide."

"His suicide? Joe died in 1945 when he was eight years old."

❖

Franklin's debrief left Morrow speechless. This couldn't be a coincidence. Too many clues tied Joseph Chandler back to the old woman in Riverside. The only remaining logical explanation was also the least rational: The Eastlake hermit found dead in his bathroom had been living under a stolen identity.

To be certain, Morrow phoned the library in Sherman, Texas. According to Kaaber's account, this was the midsized city in northern Texas where her little cousin—the real Joe Chandler—had lost his life in a car accident fifty-seven years ago. She remembered that tragedy had struck on or around Christmas Eve. A librarian agreed to search the county's press archives, where she found a news clipping from the local paper that seemed to match his story.

On the evening of December 21, 1945, Joseph Newton Chandler II, forty-four years old, his wife Ellen Chandler née Kaaber, thirty-three years old, and their son Joseph Newton Chandler III, eight years old, had been driving on a country road in the western suburbs of Dallas. The father, a salesman for an automobile company, was driving their Buick sedan, which was filled with gifts. As was their annual tradition, the family had left their home in Tulsa, Oklahoma, to spend the holidays with little Joe's paternal grandmother in Weatherford, Texas, the Chandlers' hometown.

It was a clear night, and the roads were relatively quiet. A pair of headlights appeared on the horizon from a massive truck loaded with lumber and headed in the opposite direction. As the vehicles were about to pass each other, the truck driver swerved and crossed into their lane. He was unable to correct course in time. The impact of the head-on collision could be compared to a train moving at full speed and slamming into a moped. It decimated the Buick, and the Chandlers died instantly. The truck driver and the friend who was with him in the cabin were uninjured.

Of the thousand questions that crossed Morrow's mind, two stood out from the rest. How long had this elderly man lived under a fake name, and how had he pulled it off? Morrow kept on digging and got a hold of John Doe's death certificate, which featured his social security number. In the United States, social security numbers and cards are issued upon request to people of working age, which means they can't be granted before the applicant is sixteen or seventeen.

Next, Morrow contacted the US Social Security Administration to get a copy of the application for this number. Jackpot. The applicant had submitted the form on September 25, 1978, at a branch in Rapid City, South Dakota. Most notably, the civil status provided by the applicant was a perfect match with the boy who had died in 1945, including the names and places of birth of his parents.

Morrow no longer had any doubts.

Little Joseph Chandler had lost his life at a young age, and someone else had lived that life instead.

PART 2
1823 CENTER STREET

Chapter 4

"Fuck me, fuck me, fuck me running."

When Tom Doyle was about to launch into a good story, a funny anecdote, he always had this greedy grin on his face. It was the look of a guy thinking about the punchline before even starting the joke. But when he was about to drop a bombshell, something truly shocking, he would say "Fuck me, fuck me, fuck me running," while pacing and shaking his head as though he couldn't believe it himself.

It was time for the morning briefing. Doyle had gathered Bowersock, Kroczak, and his other detectives in front of a large whiteboard in a meeting room. Everyone understood they would have to wait before getting their assignments for the day.

"Guys, you're not gonna believe this." Doyle explained that the day before, he had gotten a call from Judge Klammer. This was already surprising in itself, as the judge should technically have contacted him through the chief of police, according to the chain of command, but it was urgent. Klammer was in his office with a man named Larry Morrow, the private investigator who specialized in finding heirs and who had looked into the Chandler case. According to him, the Dover Place guy had been living under a stolen identity—not for fifteen days but for *twenty-four years*.

"So, who is this guy?" Bowersock thought out loud.

"That's what we're gonna try and find out."

Lieutenant Doyle's first initiative was to check that the fake Joseph Chandler wasn't registered to WITSEC, a program that assigns new identities to protect government witnesses in federal cases. In these instances, the Department of Justice determines whether a witness may benefit from the program, but implementation is managed by the US Marshals, whose regular duties include tracking down fugitives and escorting prisoners.

Doyle called Peter Elliott in his Cleveland office. They'd known each other since the early 1990s, and Elliott had just been appointed as the head US marshal for the northern district of Ohio. When they had first crossed paths, Doyle was a rank-and-file patrol officer in Eastlake, and Elliott was a new investigator with the local Bureau of Alcohol, Tobacco, Firearms and Explosives, a federal unit specializing in cases of firearms and explosives trafficking.

The city of Cleveland was a small community in which judiciary and law enforcement authorities all eventually worked together on topics of common interest, forging lifelong relationships. A brief search confirmed that no WITSEC participant had ever registered under that name.

With this lead out of the way, Doyle started casting lines in all directions. The first step, the most economical in terms of both time and money, was reaching out to the press. Doyle gave an interview to the Lake County *News-Herald* and *The Plain Dealer*. The latter had a readership of roughly one hundred thousand and soon published an article titled "But who is this guy, really?" with a photo of Chandler's driver's license. The story caught the attention of the national media, including TV stations, and teams of reporters were sent out to cover the ghost hunt. The local paper in Rapid City, where the fraudster had applied for a social security card that marked the beginning of his second life, went so far as to create an age-regression photo suggesting what he might have looked like in 1978 to stir up potential memories among its readers.

It was a good story and even made it across the Atlantic, where Doyle was invited to tell the tale of his investigation to the BBC. "Every time the story is picked up, we have a chance to solve this," he explained to a reporter from *The Plain Dealer*. "I don't think it will be in England, but you never know."

The summer of 2003 was the start of a second, more technical phase of the investigation. All exhibits collected in the Dover Place studio D were pulled out of storage for analysis. The list of evidence held in the station's basement was long: one five-shot revolver and the four bullets remaining in the cylinder, one gun case, one plastic bag filled with fifteen loose .38-caliber cartridges, a dozen cards in a wallet (municipal library, organ donation, car insurance...), a set of seven keys found in the deceased man's pants, one pair of large eyeglasses, one calendar, and one Seiko SQ watch, which was one of the first Japanese quartz models and thus a symbol of avant-garde style and high tech.

The inventory also included the two books that had been left prominently on the desk and that Formick, the crime scene tech, had packed away, assuming a suicide note might be tucked in between the pages—this did not turn out to be the case. And lastly, there was one small safe. Some hoped the contents of the safe would provide a solid clue to help solve the mystery, but once cracked, it was found to contain only bank statements, check stubs, and other papers and trinkets of no interest.

On Doyle's orders, each piece of sealed evidence was taken, one after the other, to the county crime lab for fingerprinting. There were so many items that he eagerly awaited results, feeling confident.

But not a single fingerprint was found on any of the evidence.

One last hope remained. Maybe they could make the old GMC pickup talk. The vehicle had been at a pound since the day Chandler's body was found and would remain there until the green light was given to have it destroyed. Surely the owner would have left behind at least one print. Formick was methodical, even pulling the ashtray from the dashboard so the lab could examine it separately. Like Doyle, he noted in passing that it was overflowing with butts even though nobody had ever seen Chandler smoke. Then he tested the entire cab for fingerprints through cyanoacrylate fuming, a process that uses vaporized superglue to detect latent prints within thirty minutes.

No prints were found anywhere.

It was as though this man had worn gloves all day, every day, or at least in the last few months preceding his suicide.

By early 2005, after two years of investigation, all that remained were letters from oddballs who thought they recognized their missing son or brother-in-law in Joseph Chandler's photo. Some of the more outlandish letters claimed that Chandler resembled the elusive and mythical Zodiac Killer.

Feeling as though he had put in a reasonable amount of effort given the relative importance of the case, Doyle let this one go cold. At the end of the day, the biggest mistake had been to authorize cremation too soon, which made it impossible to retrieve a genetic sample. At the time that the body was found in 2002, DNA analysis had been a fledgling technique and not yet an integral part of police procedures. And how could anyone have imagined what would come next?

On January 15, 2008, the probate court officially closed its part of the Chandler case, putting an end to the search for heirs. Of the $60,000 in cash belonging to the deceased, $50,000 had been used by the court to finance this search. In accordance with the law, the remaining $10,000 was turned over to the state.

By the time he retired in 2011, Lieutenant Doyle was leaving behind such a long and successful career that he didn't consider the Chandler case a failure. When tackling investigations, he had always been fueled by a desire to deliver justice. And although it was fascinating, the enigma of this unnamed retiree had claimed no victims.

One man did not share Tom Doyle's point of view: Peter Elliott, the US marshal for the northern district of Ohio. Or rather, he found this conclusion premature. As long as this man's identity remained a mystery, how could the authorities be sure he hadn't caused anyone any harm?

On April 8, 2014, Elliott stepped into the modest Eastlake police station. Since his appointment twelve years prior by President George W. Bush, this was the first time he'd visited in person. "We'd like to take a look at this file, see if we can help," he told the chief of police before showing up. The warning was a courtesy, expressing his intention to take over the investigation. Earlier that year, Elliott had created a special unit for cold cases. To the detectives gathered in the meeting room, he presented his hunch—this strange case had to be hiding a bigger mystery, something more significant, that was worth solving. No one up and changes their identity halfway through their life just for kicks. No one locks up their past so carefully that even death won't deliver the key.

By erasing the man he once was from the archives of history, this John Doe had wanted to take something with him to the grave.

Chapter 5

Kathleen, Vita Ebbert's assistant, never tallied the number of residents she'd moved in, but Dover Place records show that in her six years spent as the assistant manager on the property, she must have processed about two hundred new arrivals. It was impossible for her to remember every tenant, but she'd never quite forgotten Joseph Chandler.

He had first contacted her by phone after seeing an ad in the newspaper. According to procedure, he had to sign the lease in the Dover Place office and move into the apartment on the same day. In the registration form filled out a few days prior, Joseph Chandler had listed himself as single and forty-eight years old. He had likely arrived in the area recently because he told Kathleen he had been staying at the Knights Inn, a low-end local motel, for the past week.

To avoid any discrimination in the tenant selection process, the form was sent to a third-party company for approval. They accepted his application despite one comment: The applicant had a low credit score, a sign of a chaotic banking history. This was unexpected for a Lubrizol employee who claimed to be paid $17.75 an hour, which was more than five times the federal minimum wage.

On October 22, 1985, with the lease signed, Kathleen handed the studio D key to its new occupant and walked over to the unit with him. Although the apartment walkthrough was by no means a formal event, Mr. Chandler had made a point of dressing in style with dark pants and a crisp white shirt. He was a small man, his hair already gray, but she was most struck by the man's exceptionally taciturn nature. During the entire visit, he did not speak one word. Tenants were often curious about their new environment, and even the quietest ones always had at least one question to ask. *Are there dryers available? How does the heating work? Where can you get good pizza nearby?*

Apartment tours typically lasted a solid hour. This one had taken half as long, and Kathleen figured he'd set a record. She hadn't really felt uncomfortable or afraid, but it must have been unsettling to spend thirty minutes talking to someone who refused to open his mouth.

For the next seventeen years, Joseph Chandler did not interact with any of his neighbors. He was never seen hosting a visitor—man, woman, or child. Whenever he left the property, it was either to go to work or to have breakfast at Nick's, a family restaurant about a quarter mile away, where the walls were plastered with photos of sailboats. And once he retired in 1997, he simply stopped leaving his home altogether, except for his daily one-hour walk through the property in the late morning or early afternoon. He was always well dressed, wearing an ironed shirt and pants, and would walk in the shade of the Dover Place elm trees with a mechanical gait, his gaze set straight ahead, indifferent to the world.

The only Dover Place resident who ever heard the sound of his voice was Jeffrey Offak, the head of maintenance. Offak lived on site, in employee housing, and was perpetually walking up and down the tree-lined footpaths with his toolbox in hand.

Amid the chaos of residents constantly coming and going, Offak was a familiar face. When he crossed paths with Chandler, he'd offer a "hello" and a wave. Chandler would return the greeting, without the wave, as long as courtesy didn't compel him to alter his course.

When the tenant from apartment D showed up in his office, their interactions were equally brief. It typically happened two or three times a year, especially on sunny days. Chandler would come in complaining that his apartment was infested with fleas and that Offak had to spray the place down. He never expressed anger, just stated the facts. "Look, I'm covered in bites," he'd mumble as he showed Offak his arms, his voice practically a whisper. Offak would spend a moment staring at his arms, without ever finding a hint of a bite. Still, he'd reassure the tenant: "I'll take care of it." The first few times, he dutifully sprayed the apartment, but Chandler kept coming back. After a while, though, Offak continued promising to resolve the issue but stopped doing anything, and Chandler never complained.

In retrospect, Dover Place was the perfect home base for someone looking to build a secret life. The place offered no opportunity to build community, given the high turnover rate in the two hundred twenty-nine units. The property was located by a stretch of road along which people only stopped to change a flat tire. It was close to Lake Erie but not close enough that residents would cross paths with a wayward boater. The police station was less than half a mile away. Far enough to be out of sight and close enough that officers would drive by the property ten times a day and stop noticing it altogether.

The fact that Chandler chose Eastlake doesn't seem like a total coincidence either. First, the geographical location lent itself to anonymity. Fanning out in a crescent shape along the shores of Lake Erie, Eastlake was split down the middle by a marina. This small harbor divided the town into two isolated neighborhoods in which people tended to stay put. There was no downtown core where gossip would be exchanged, and residents had to travel three miles to Willoughby for the nearest busy commercial strip. Eastlake wasn't really a city—where everything is seen—but it was not quite the countryside either—where everything is known. To the west, Cleveland was a twenty-minute drive along Interstate 90, and it took just as long headed east to start seeing the first red barns, a typical sight in Ohio fields and in rural horror movies.

It's also easier to be forgotten in a city that has remained in history's blind spot. Every American city holds a record, most often related to its past. When Eastlake had no record, the town created its own claim to fame: a line of five hundred American flags installed around the town hall, the largest display of its kind in the country.

And as Cleveland was pivoting to the service economy, Eastlake held on to the region's industrial roots, epitomized by the town's coal-fired power station, built by the lake and prominently featuring a six-hundred-foot smokestack reminiscent of an old rusty lighthouse. Day and night, it spewed clouds of ash that rained down on cars and houses and left a whiff of white-hot barbecue on the breeze. The effects of the plant were most obvious in winter when the snow would be blanketed in black tar.

Locals learned to live with it. After all, the company cleaned the roads several times a year, at their own expense, and no one could forget that the power station was by far the top employer in town, with three hundred fifty workers who were treated much better than their ancestors and who took home a much fatter paycheck. In fact, Eastlake residents had coal taxes to thank for their low municipal taxes and for the local high school that looked like an Ivy League campus.

A town like a thousand others, Eastlake was the perfect example of a white working-class America that had been lifted to middle class by economic growth while still embracing its blue-collar DNA. This was an America where people double-parked their pickup trucks and left the engine running while they ran out for a pack of gum and Marlboros. Where people only took the stairs when the elevator was out of order. Where grocery stores played the best of Bon Jovi on repeat and relegated water bottles to the back of the fridge. Where hunting rifles were advertised on roadside billboards.

Aside from weekend outings in one of the two local bars, which were often packed, people were happy to stay home and spend time with a close circle of friends, without looking to broaden their horizons. This was a town where comfort and practicality reigned supreme. When people voted Republican or Democrat, they based their decision on the latest hot-button issues, not on ideology. Routine was not so much a sign of boredom as a clear indicator of success. In this context, strangers were neither intruders nor a source of curiosity. They could do whatever they wanted as long as they didn't bother anyone.

To live a life hidden in plain sight, you couldn't find a better place than Eastlake, Ohio.

Lubrizol employees had more detailed recollections of Chandler than the people from the Dover Place

Apartments. And they were more disconcerting. His former colleagues recalled a man with an impeccable appearance despite an occasionally questionable body odor. They claimed they hadn't shunned their timid colleague, but rather it was Chandler who seemed reluctant to interact. When people spoke to him without warning or when he was bothered by a nearby conversation, he would slip on a pair of headphones and switch on a black box in his pocket. Though everyone had initially assumed it was a Walkman, it turned out to be a white noise machine that he had made himself. According to researchers, this random mix of frequencies, sounding like a poorly tuned AM radio station, was found to have a calming effect on subjects. Every time he used it, Chandler would set the device to max volume. He didn't go anywhere without it.

In addition to confirming his reclusive tendencies, the anecdote also showed that Chandler had a knack for tinkering, a fact that was echoed in other stories. In his spare time, he had built himself an electronic box that he hooked up to his TV. The device had the power to turn off the TV at the start of each commercial break and then turn it back on when the ads were over. It was the first ad blocker ever made. He abhorred all forms of advertising.

When Chandler's office neighbors found out about his genius invention, they immediately requested their own, which he agreed to make for a few bucks. And when a colleague who was a volunteer firefighter asked for help, Chandler brought his electrical kit to the firehouse, where he improved the overnight warning system by adding a new function: As soon as the siren went off, the lights would automatically turn on in the sleeping area.

Chandler's unwillingness to speak made him a peculiar character, but when he finally did open his mouth, he was downright bizarre.

One Monday morning at the office, he arrived upset about a mishap that had occurred over the weekend. He told his colleagues that, on a whim, he had decided to go shopping at L.L.Bean. The company had about fifty stores across the United States and sold equipment for campers and hunters. One of the locations was about ten miles from Eastlake, but Chandler specifically wanted to go to the larger, historic Freeport store, which was open 24-7.

But Freeport wasn't just around the corner. The city was in Maine, a 740-mile, twelve-hour drive east of Eastlake—and that's not counting pit stops. So Chandler had simply made the drive there in his old pickup truck. But once in Freeport, he'd found that the parking lot was full. Rather than wait patiently, he immediately turned around and drove back to Ohio, covering 1,500 miles in one weekend—for nothing. "If I can't park easily, I'm keeping my money," he commented, still angry over the trip.

The other slice of life he saw fit to share with his office mates was no less strange. He told them how he was invited to a Halloween party one time. Chandler knew it was customary to dress up for such events, but he had opted to wear a shirt and pants, his usual work attire. At the party, the host made a comment about it, to which he replied, "You're mistaken, I am wearing a costume. I'm dressed up as a Lubrizol electrician." What was meant to be a good joke ended up leaving his audience deeply perplexed.

Of all the people to have crossed Chandler's path, Mike Onderisin is the only one who attributed his eccentricities to a socially maladjusted personality. He felt for Chandler, and while he never established a sincere friendship, he figured he could at least treat him with kindness. With his wife Marilyn's consent, he invited "Joe" over for a Thanksgiving dinner one year. After Chandler's death, the couple had only vague recollections of the evening, but they did recall that their guest had been rather reserved. Over dinner, he'd shared that he was once married to a Cuban woman when he lived in Florida, though he didn't elaborate on the context and did not explain why it had ended.

The awkward dinner experience was not repeated. But Chandler showed up once more at the Onderisin home in the spring of 1992 when they threw a party for Marilyn's fiftieth birthday. The invitation was no special privilege, as Mike had invited all his Lubrizol colleagues. It was a costume party, and people were encouraged to dress up however they wanted. This time, Joseph did not try to be funny. Or perhaps he did, showing up dressed as a mob boss: black fedora, dark pinstripe jacket and pants, black shirt, white tie, cigar. The costume was unsettlingly realistic if you ignored the oversized glasses that significantly undermined the authority of this supposed leader of the underworld. His presence in itself was already a surprise. Nobody, not the Onderisins nor Chandler's colleagues, would have bet a dollar on his attendance at an event this big. And, as usual, he didn't say a word all evening.

Mike never saw Chandler again after he left Lubrizol in 1997—except one time. In March of 2002, four months before his suicide, Chandler called and asked him to come to Dover to help fill out some paperwork.

His voice had always lacked emotion, but that day, he spoke like a shadow of his former self. At the studio apartment, Mike found that his colleague had become frail, and every movement seemed to sap what little strength he had left. Chandler explained that he had just been released from the hospital. He had colon cancer and had undergone an operation that ultimately would not increase his odds of survival. Doctors were suggesting chemotherapy, but the surgery and hospital stay had cost him $80,000, and he could no longer afford the treatment. And anyway, he had no interest in taking drugs that would knock him flat. Clearly, he didn't have much time left.

Mike couldn't bear to see him give up. What if he applied for Medicare? It was pointless, Chandler told him. He was looking pale, had trouble hearing, and his mediocre eyesight had further deteriorated. Chandler had only allowed himself to ask for help because he was unable to fill out the form for his new lease and the updated emergency contact form. When Mike Onderisin picked up the form, he saw the name of this woman he did not know, "Vita Ebbert," and her profession, "Dover Property Manager." Chandler was so alone that this property manager had been promoted to the rank of a close relative.

"Let's add my name," suggested Onderisin.

And that's how he ended up getting dragged into this whole mess.

Before Onderisin left, Joseph spoke to him one last time. "I have something to tell you," he whispered. His voice was barely audible, but the sentence itself clearly carried a solemn weight. It was as though he meant to share something truly shocking. Or make an unexpected revelation. Or hand over the key to his strange personality.

For just a moment.

"No, I'll tell you some other time."

There never was another time.

Wherever he went, Joseph Chandler always carried around a black briefcase. In his studio apartment, it was found on the carpet between the computer and the sofa. At Lubrizol, he'd leave it clearly visible in a corner of his office. Onderisin had always assumed his solitary colleague was a kind of free man who shunned social convention, avoided materialism and responsibility, and was ready to board a plane at any given moment to start a new life somewhere else. If this picture had been accurate, the briefcase likely would have contained the bare essentials in case he suddenly felt the need to leave everything behind.

In fact, Chandler sometimes did disappear. He'd skip town and stop showing up for work. This would go on for several weeks, sometimes months. And then, one morning, he'd be back at his desk as if nothing had ever happened.

Before disappearing, he never told people where he was going or for how long. But to his curious colleagues, he confessed the reason for his exile in a whisper: "They're getting close."

Chapter 6

Peter Elliott's twelfth-floor office provided a sweeping view of the Cuyahoga River estuary. At the foot of downtown Cleveland's Municipal Courts Tower, the river, which perhaps had once harbored hopes of scattering into the infinite ocean, finally flowed into the dead-end reservoir that was Lake Erie. There was no better allegory to illustrate the dismay Elliott's "clients" came to feel; any fugitive who thought they were out of the woods had a marshal on their tail, determined to undermine their dreams of freedom.

Wanted suspects and witnesses, escaped convicts, people who failed to appear in court or violated parole. . . . Since his appointment in 2002 as the United States marshal for the northern district of Ohio, Elliott and his team had caught thirty-two thousand fugitives with local or federal arrest warrants in the forty counties under his jurisdiction. This degree of efficacy likely explains his unprecedented longevity in the jurisdiction. Despite being appointed by Bush Junior and despite his rumored conservative leanings, Elliott was reappointed in 2009 by Barack Obama with the unanimous support of the Senate.

His political flexibility reflected a nuanced personality. His affable manners and slicked-back short hair were reminiscent of a Don Johnson just back from Miami Beach, paired with the sharp attention of a Texas Ranger ready to draw his weapon. And although his warm handshake was friendly, his icy green eyes always seemed to be assessing the person standing before him. He also pursued a diverse range of hobbies, from baseball—an injury prevented him from going pro—to playing bagpipes, which he did with his father, a former marshal himself, in the Cleveland police's Pipes and Drums Band.

"Let no guilty man escape." Peter Elliott adopted the US Marshals' motto, with his own twist: "That extends beyond death." This is why, in early 2014, he set up a cold case unit. Behind each unsolved crime, he knew there was a fugitive on the run. Now in charge of the investigation into the unidentified Eastlake man, Elliott reviewed the three hundred pages of police records and made one first observation that justified reopening the case and making it a priority: In twenty-four years spent living under a false identity, the fake Joseph Chandler had never made even the slightest mistake. This was not insignificant.

In the United States, identity theft was rampant, though it had been in decline since 2001 due to the introduction of more strict administrative policies in the wake of the 9/11 attacks. Before this turning point, starting a second life may not have been child's play, but it was relatively straightforward. And while countries like France assigned a national ID card to every resident, this type of system did not exist across the Atlantic. In fact, identity theft in itself—when committed without any associated offenses—was not even a crime in the United States until 1998. Many magazines and books published in the 1970s, often inspired by anarchists and survivalists, even explained how to go about it, leveraging these bureaucratic loopholes and the right to freedom of expression, as protected by the First Amendment.

1.   Roam through cemeteries in search of a
     dead person to be resurrected. The prime

target: a child, born the same year as you, if possible, who died young enough to have left only a meager paper trail.

2. Contact the vital records office in the city of birth and request a copy of the birth certificate. Now comes the delicate part. A conscientious civil servant will ask for a piece of identification, like a driver's license, passport, or social security card, to avoid handing over a document that might then be used to start a new life. Without proof of identification, the employee is allowed to issue a copy of the birth certificate, but they need to stamp it with the words "not for ID purposes."

3. To get around this issue, tell them that your wallet was stolen, along with all your ID cards. If the employee servant is a zealot, try to bribe them with a fifty or a hundred-dollar bill. Public servants earn a paltry salary, so this will usually do the trick.

4. With your stolen birth certificate, apply for a social security number.

This approach, coupled with an American culture that defaults to trusting citizens, resulted in a surprisingly high success rate. But in Elliott's long career, he had found that identity thieves always ended up making a mistake. The potential missteps were wide-ranging. Sometimes, people couldn't resist the urge to contact a friend or close relative from their previous life, even just once a year, or they distractedly filled out a form with their original address. Others might tell a story from their past while out drinking. Even when they had strong support systems, the best offenders managed to stay under the radar for six months, one year, two years, or maybe five years if they were quite skilled.

But this fake Joseph Chandler had not tripped up for almost a quarter century, until his very last breath.

For Elliott, this feat provided two insights that would guide his investigation. The first was that this man had taken extreme, continuous, and extraordinary care to live under the radar, freeing himself from the slightest friendly or emotional attachment and thus avoiding being exposed. Hence the second lesson: Such a degree of precaution had to be hiding a troubled past.

The past of a serious criminal, no doubt.

As he pored over police records, Elliott lamented—as Tom Doyle had before him—the premature cremation of the remains. What he found even harder to accept was the lack of any autopsy records. To check if perhaps the document was simply missing, he called the Cleveland coroner, Dr. Rizzo, who had received the body on July 30, 2002. Rizzo confirmed that he had not thoroughly examined the deceased. The entry and exit wounds in the head were consistent with a .38-caliber bullet fired into the mouth, so he'd been satisfied with just a visual examination. On paper, he had jotted down his observations as well as some anatomical data like height, weight, and that sort of thing. He had also carried out a dental examination and kept a copy of his findings.

Elliott was taken aback by this casual approach to the forensics component of the case. To put it plainly, the only indisputable material evidence he possessed to try and match the Eastlake stranger with a wanted fugitive was a diagram of the deceased man's jaw, a list of teeth that were missing or present, and a brief description of their condition.

At any given moment, the number of fugitives on the run in the United States was roughly two million. In addition to this already astronomical scope, Elliott wanted to widen his search to include the pool of roughly twenty thousand missing persons. Most of them were runaway teens who were quickly located, but it also included a fair share of adults who had simply vanished into thin air.

The database was online and available to members of law enforcement on a dedicated platform in which each file included a physical description, sometimes a photo, and the circumstances of the disappearance. Though Elliott was convinced he was dealing with a former criminal on the run, there was no guarantee that this man was suspected of the offense he had committed or that the said offense was even known to the police and the subject of an investigation. In the eyes of the law, this unidentified man might be a missing person case, one among thousands.

This left him no choice but to conduct a manual search. Elliott's team would have to develop theories and then verify and rule out each one. It was a labyrinth with two million points of entry, and only one would lead them to the exit. Elliott started by searching the fugitive database in his jurisdiction, then expanded the scope to include the Most Wanted lists from the other ninety-three US Marshals offices across the United States. Lastly, he included the FBI's Most Wanted fugitives.

In his search, the first criterion was purely physical. Elliott focused on faces that bore some resemblance to the unnamed retiree. Next, he filtered results by using the other attributes of the deceased. According to Dr. Rizzo, Chandler was five feet seven, and although he had not weighed the body, the 160 pounds listed on his driver's license seemed to fit. Because a person's height and weight will vary over their lifetime, Elliott gave himself a margin of error.

The man's age remained an enigma, but experience had shown Elliott that, on this point as on many others, identity thieves tended to stay close to reality. Little Joe Chandler was born in 1937, so the fake Chandler was likely a contemporary.

To these objective criteria, Elliott added a few more subjective points based on the profile he was building. His best candidate was likely a fugitive known to suffer from OCD, as demonstrated by the stories about the white noise device and the imaginary flea infestations in studio D, and someone with a more than above-average intelligence.

Elliott started by focusing on states that were somehow tied to the case, even if it was a tenuous connection. There was Ohio, of course, and Texas, the home of the real Chandler family, and California. In his social security application forms, Chandler had listed several former employers, and although the investigation showed he had never worked at any of these companies, the clue suggested that he had likely lived nearby for at least some time.

The northern district of California US Marshals' home page featured the artificially aged faces of three octogenarians. Elliott was familiar with these fugitives and even knew what they had looked like when they were younger. Every marshal worth his salt remembered them; they were the legendary Alcatraz escapees. And one of the men in the artificially aged photos, Frank Morris, bore an uncanny resemblance to the Eastlake retiree. Both had the same high and wide forehead and the same thin, pursed lips. Their expressions were a bit different, with Morris looking more stern than Chandler, but the prominent nose and wide nostrils were similar. Elliott clicked on the profile.

The arrest warrant issued by the state of California had been out since June 11, 1962. It listed his weight, 135 pounds, which was irrelevant because too much time had gone by. His height was five feet, eight inches, only one inch taller than Chandler. It was close, but it would take something more significant to turn the marshal's curiosity into excitement. Online, myriad articles described Frank Morris's life and personality. One detail came up again and again: The man had an IQ of 133, better than 98 percent of Americans.

Just a few weeks after Elliott took over the Chandler case, he got a sign that he was on the right track.

He immediately flew to San Francisco. If Chandler had been one of America's most famous fugitives—their sensational escape from the Alcatraz Federal Penitentiary gave rise to hundreds of books and articles and inspired a cinematic masterpiece with Clint Eastwood in the role of Frank Morris—it would certainly have justified going to great lengths to remain under the radar.

Morris had been a serial bank robber and was considered the mastermind behind this wild plan. For months, the three men had used improvised tools to widen the ventilation ducts in their cells, leading to an unguarded utility corridor. In this space, they built a makeshift raft out of fifty stolen raincoats so they could reach the mainland. After their escape, the police concluded that they had drowned in the icy waters of San Francisco Bay despite the fact that the raft was never found. The US Marshals, true to their motto "Let no guilty man escape," never stopped searching for these legendary fugitives.

Over the phone, Elliott's Californian counterpart had been intrigued, but not overly excited, by this fresh lead. When they met in person, he acknowledged the coincidence but suggested it wasn't quite enough to be conclusive. He promised that they would look into the lead but also shared that the case wasn't at a standstill; the investigation had just taken a new turn. It was clear to Elliott that a better lead than his own must have recently come to light, so he flew back to Cleveland.

He continued to spend hours scrolling through online fugitive profiles while also digging for new clues. In the hope of finding some detail that had been overlooked, he went back to interview witnesses like Mike Onderisin, who had already spoken with the police, and reached out to people who had not yet been heard, such as Jeffrey Offak, the Dover Place service manager.

An ex-colleague told Elliott that, in addition to the story of the Cuban wife, Chandler had confessed to having been married to a Catholic woman, without further clarification. Had he been married twice? Was this the same woman? Had he ever been married? He found no answers, only more questions.

Research into the handgun used for the suicide turned out to be more fruitful. The serial number on the gun, a Charter 2000 short-barrel revolver, led Elliott to a gun shop near Eastlake. The .38-caliber handgun had been legally purchased for $263 in April 2002, three months before Chandler's suicide.

In the summer of 2014, as a result of his tedious work, Elliott managed to dig up a previously unexplored lead. In an interview with Elliott, Mike Onderisin had once again described his last conversation with Chandler, four months before his death, in his studio apartment. He explained that Chandler, in a weakened state, had told him he had rectal cancer, for which he'd recently undergone surgery. Bingo! Where there had been an operation, there had to be a medical record. And while hospital records might not tell him who their John Doe really was, it would cost him nothing to contact the two local hospitals.

He found that the medical center in Willoughby, a city bordering Eastlake, did have a file under the name Joseph Chandler. A cooperative administrative employee agreed to look into the case.

She told Elliott that, according to the hospital archives, Chandler had in fact been to the hospital twice. The first, a brief visit, had been on February 4, 1989. That day, Joseph Chandler had gone to the emergency room for an unusual reason: a fairly severe penile injury. A nurse examined him and was astonished to find he had lacerations on his penis. Some of the cuts were quite deep. When the nurse asked her patient how he had suffered the injuries, he told her that he had inserted his penis into the hose of his vacuum cleaner for sexual play and that things had gone wrong. Chandler was treated without any kind of moral judgment.

The second hospital stay was dated March 5, 2000. The hospital employee confirmed that the patient had in fact undergone a surgical procedure to treat a malignant tumor on his colon. The diagnosis had been made shortly before the operation and was based on a biopsy.

"Oh, and if it helps with the investigation," she added, "we kept a tissue sample."

Chapter 7

When Peter Elliott stumbled across an online *Seattle Times* article about the Lori Kennedy case in September 2016, he uttered a quiet, "Oh my God!" The story was practically the same as the Chandler case, which had eluded him for two years, or almost fifteen years if you included the futile efforts of the Eastlake police investigators who preceded him.

But what truly shocked him was the realization that, unlike the Chandler case, the Lori Kennedy mystery had just been solved.

On Christmas morning in 2010, Lori Kennedy, a newly divorced woman in her forties, was found unresponsive in the driver's seat of her car in the small town of Longview, Texas. She had killed herself with a bullet to the head. In the family home, inside a closet that her ex-husband had been forbidden to open, her relatives found a metal box labeled "Crafts." Inside was one single document: a July 1988 Dallas court decision authorizing Becky Sue Turner to change her name to Lori Kennedy.

Except that Becky Sue Turner was not her real name either. It was the name of a two-year-old girl who had died in 1971 in a house fire at her parents' home near Seattle. Lori had stolen her identity in early 1988 by applying for a social security number in her name, using a copy of the child's birth certificate. It was the method described in the anarchist textbooks—the same one that the fake Joseph Chandler had used a decade before her.

So who was Lori Kennedy, really? The police had her DNA but found it matched none of their records. For a while, it seemed as though the truth about her past would be lost for good. Then Colleen Fitzpatrick entered the picture. She was a scientist from New Orleans who, at the age of fifty, had ended her career as a physicist to pursue full-time genealogy, her favorite hobby. When direct-to-consumer DNA testing websites first came on the scene, she immediately began using these databases, which compiled millions of DNA profiles, to build or fill out family trees. The practice became known as "genetic genealogy." With her company Identifinders

International, she became famous when she used a DNA sample from a molar to identify an anonymous *Titanic* passenger: a nineteen-month-old baby whose remains had been recovered from the North Atlantic and buried in Canada. "My approach is like *CSI Meets Genealogy*," she explained with a mischievous smile.

In 2013, when Fitzpatrick came across an article about the Lori Kennedy case, she figured she could help solve the mystery. With law enforcement buy-in, she sent the unknown DNA for comparison to the three major websites that collected, analyzed, and stored the DNA profiles of millions of Americans: AncestryDNA, 23andMe, and FamilyTreeDNA. Apart from a few matches with distant cousins who were too far removed to be of any use, the search turned up nothing.

Over the next few months, Fitzpatrick regularly sent the sample back for testing again, until the search turned up a third cousin who could provide a family tree. With the help of online vital records, she then patiently moved her way up the tree to find a common ancestor between this distant cousin and Lori Kennedy. Then she moved back down the tree, branch by branch, until she identified a first cousin living in Philadelphia, Pennsylvania.

When the cousin saw Lori's driver's license photo, she immediately recognized Kimberly McLean, her aunt

Deanne's daughter. As a teen, Kim couldn't cope with her parents' divorce. One day, at the age of eighteen, she'd slammed the door on the way out of her mother's house and told them, "I'm leaving forever." She wasn't kidding.

As Elliott read this epilogue, at his computer in the fall of 2016, he felt a surge of adrenaline. The Chandler case was so similar to the Lori Kennedy story; Fitzpatrick was bound to be able to crack the code. Over the phone, she admitted she was unfamiliar with this story about the Eastlake retiree but was immediately hooked. "This is right up my alley," she said.

The DNA profile established using Joseph Chandler's biopsy tissue from 2000 was then sent to Identifinders International in California. When Fitzpatrick received the sample, she realized the genome was incomplete. The tissue sample was quite degraded, as it had been kept by the hospital in a simple block of paraffin for fifteen years. They were only able to reconstruct 7 percent of the genetic profile, which would make it harder to accurately identify family members who were still alive. Luckily, the Y-chromosome DNA, found only in males and passed down from father to son, was practically intact.

Fitzpatrick ran this Y-DNA sequencing through an online genetic database created specifically for this chromosome and got a match: one Mr. Nicholas, born in 1944 and still alive. The man didn't recognize the photo of Joseph Chandler, but he wanted to help and was able to provide a family tree that was nearly complete. It went all the way back to George Nicholas, who had left Dorset, England, in 1722 for the New World and whose family started one of the first colonies in Virginia. As Fitzpatrick moved down the tree, she identified other living Nicholas family members with DNA that matched Chandler's. Her provisional conclusion was that the male lineage was intact and traceable. This meant that the Cleveland John Doe's real last name was Nicholas or some close variation.

Still, this leap forward was actually less significant than it appeared. Pioneer George Nicholas had thousands of male descendants born around the same time as the fake Chandler. Contacting them one by one was not feasible. With only Y-DNA at her disposal, Fitzpatrick was in a bind.

In early 2017, to get around this recurring issue in her cases, Fitzpatrick teamed up with an acquaintance named Margaret Press, whom she had met on Facebook. Press was a retired computer engineer who wanted to use her talents as a programmer to support her passion for genealogy. Together, they founded the

DNA Doe Project, a nonprofit dedicated to solving cold cases through the magic of genetic genealogy. Chandler was the ideal guinea pig—a John Doe with a common last name and a degraded DNA sample. Both partners agreed that they would need to sequence the DNA sample again in the hope of obtaining a more complete genome and a better dataset than just the Y chromosome. Fitzpatrick called Peter Elliott to get his consent because handling such a degraded sample was not without risk. Green light.

The second DNA sequencing was done by a private lab in September 2017 and was hardly more exhaustive than the original one. The good news was a new online genetic database, GEDmatch, had recently been launched. Free and publicly accessible, it was less rich in data than competitors providing paid services. But, unlike these competitors, the site allowed users to upload existing DNA data files and required no saliva sample.

Among the million genetic profiles published by GEDmatch, a few hundred belonging to living people had notable similarities with the incomplete John Doe genome. The problem was neither of the Doe Project partners found anyone genetically closer than a third cousin. Still, with the help of nineteen volunteers,

Fitzpatrick and Press contacted some of these distant cousins and asked them to share their genealogy. Many enthusiastically joined in.

After three months of work, dozens of family trees were reconstructed, each with hundreds of branches. The likelihood that Joseph Chandler was linked to one of these branches was nearly 100 percent. His real name might even be listed among the hundreds of male profiles they had compiled. Yet without a better lead, stubbornly keeping at it would have amounted to pruning each branch of each tree with a nail clipper.

Fitzpatrick and Press came to the same conclusion: A third sequencing was the only way to refine the search. They figured if they couldn't get a more complete DNA sequence, this would at least allow them to identify different genetic markers. If you were to take two low-resolution photographs of the same subject at the same time, you would have two blurry images, but each one might capture a detail that the other did not. By superimposing them, you could develop a clearer picture.

It would not be an exaggeration to say this was their very last chance. The DNA sample from Chandler's biopsy had been reduced to only a tiny cluster of usable cells. After this third analysis, there would be nothing left.

As expected, this result was just as compromised. And, as expected, some known genetic markers had disappeared while other markers that had previously been invisible were now showing up.

On March 5, 2018, a geneticist with the DNA Doe Project produced a DNA supersequence combining all known markers and then uploaded it to GEDmatch for comparison. The site delivered a genetic profile that matched a cousin who was just as distant as previous matches—but his tree had yet to be reconstructed. A volunteer got to work.

In the grandparents' generation, she came across one Alpha Schreiber, who had died in 1990. Schreiber—this last name had already come up in the family tree of another distant cousin. Alpha Schreiber had married one Silas Nichols, also deceased. The couple had lived in Indiana. They had four children, all boys. Here were two family trees that shared a common relative, and especially this name, Nichols, a popular variation of Nicholas, which the Y chromosome had pointed to.

Fitzpatrick and Press tried to temper their enthusiasm but felt a home run was on the horizon. The Nichols spouses and their four sons had in fact already been identified four months prior, but nothing distinguished their branch from the vast, tangled network of family trees. Like the Eastlake John Doe, who had been hidden in plain sight, the right clue had been there all along, right under their noses.

Of Alpha and Silas Nicholses' four boys, only one was not listed as "deceased" in the civil register. His name was Robert Ivan Nichols, born September 12, 1926, in New Albany, Indiana. If he was still alive, he would have now reached the respectable age of ninety-two.

A volunteer was tasked with finding a copy of his birth certificate. The home address of the Nichols family was written in elegant cursive: 1823 Center Street, New Albany.

1823 Center Street.

One of the team members latched onto this bit of information. The address looked familiar. He repeated it in his head, over and over, as if trying to shake an apple out of a tree.

And then suddenly, bingo.

"Isn't this the bogus address in Columbus for Chandler's fake sister?"

PART 3
THE BLAST FROM
THE EXPLOSION

Chapter 8

The USS *Aaron Ward* was going in circles. For six weeks, the US Navy's destroyer minelayer had been sailing around the Pacific Ocean, about twenty miles east of Okinawa. To support American ground troops that had recently landed on the island, the 2,200-ton steelcraft had been patrolling the area. In the Pacific War, Okinawa was the last strategic stronghold still in the hands of Emperor Hirohito. If the Americans could control it, Tokyo would be within bombing range. By this date, the outcome mattered only to the two warring nations. The rest of the world was processing the news that Adolf Hitler had died, cornered in his bunker. In five days, Nazi Germany would surrender, while the United States and Japan would continue to wage this two-nation world war, as if settling one last personal matter.

On Thursday, May 3, 1945, the sky was especially clear with not a cloud or enemy aircraft on the horizon. Commander Bill Sanders's ship cruised at twelve knots over calm waters. Aboard the destroyer, the three hundred crew members took this opportunity to read, play cards, and write to their fiancées. Over the past month and a half, the Battle of Okinawa had already cost the Americans twenty out of the roughly one hundred destroyers they had deployed. All had been sunk by kamikaze attacks. So far, the USS *Aaron Ward* had emerged unscathed from nine suicide attacks after managing to shoot down the Japanese aircraft before they reached their target. The crew's composure was especially remarkable given that most of the sailors had recently volunteered to serve.

Whenever the alarm sounded, all crew members were to climb up to the ship's turrets. The rest of the time, each man had his own job to attend to. Above deck was the command room, equipped with radars and communication tools, as well as sleeping quarters, kitchens, the mess deck, and the laundry room.

Below deck was the realm of the "black gang," a group of machine operators with soot-smeared faces.

One group was assigned to the engine room, while the other worked in the fire room, feeding a furnace that powered the ship's massive steam turbines. The fire room was commanded by three experienced officers, a unit that consisted of sixteen sailors. Among them was second-class Robert Nichols from New Albany, Indiana. He was a young high school student, and this was his first mission since he had voluntarily enlisted in May of 1944. He was only eighteen years old.

At 6:22 P.M., the radar operator noticed a blinking dot on the green screen that aroused him from his torpor. Could it be a flock of geese? He'd already been fooled once before, sounding the alarm and resulting in twenty-six guns aimed at a few untroubled birds traveling in a V formation. The dot disappeared. Then it reappeared in a series of more insistent beeps. The bogey was sixty miles south of the ship and headed their way at a speed of roughly 185 miles per hour. This was no goose.

"Battle stations!" the quartermaster boomed as he sounded the alarm. The men who had been resting darted out of their bunks, leaving behind open books and spilled cups of coffee. Young Nichols and the rest of the "black gang" scaled the ladders up to the gun turrets, as did all members of the crew. On the bridge, the atmosphere was tense. "Someone's going to catch hell tonight," whispered an officer.

At 6:29 P.M., a dark pinpoint appeared before the setting sun. A Japanese light bomber was approaching at full speed, less than six miles away. At the front of the ship, the two battery guns swung around to face it in one synchronized motion. Behind one of these guns, Robert Nichols waited, a human link in the ammunition supply chain.

The aircraft was only four miles away when they were ordered to open fire. Ten seconds later, black smoke billowed out of the target. But it was too soon to celebrate; the damaged airplane initiated a slow glide toward the ship. The gunners continued to fire, now aiming for the wings, in the hopes of accelerating the descent. The plane finally met its end in a plume of foam and salt water less than a hundred yards from the deck. A piece of the engine burst out of the water and ricocheted off Nichols's turret, though it caused no casualties.

The radar immediately picked up a second approaching aircraft. All men had remained at their posts—suicide attacks were never isolated. This time, the enemy was neutralized from a safe distance and disappeared into the sea. But one of the twin-mount antiaircraft guns kept on firing. A gunner had spotted a third plane on the horizon before the radar operator had picked it up. A 450-pound bomb hung from its fuselage. Dodging a barrage of gunfire, the pilot initiated a suicide dive. He was finally struck less than four miles from the ship but managed to maintain a glide on his destructive mission. "We're not going to get him!" yelled a gunner at the aft end of the ship.

A moment later, he was thrown from his station when two explosions rocked the steel behemoth in quick succession. The pilot had dropped the bomb a few yards before impact, striking the hull below the waterline, while the plane crashed into the ship's superstructure. As water rushed into the engine room through a gash nearly fifty feet long, above deck, thick black smoke poured out of the burning plane, blinding the survivors who stumbled over mangled bodies.

But things were about to get much worse for the destroyer. Over the next fifty minutes, the USS *Aaron Ward* was the target of seven more kamikaze attacks, five of which hit their target. By the time the USS *Shannon* arrived to tow the ship, their spotlights swept across nothing more than a tangle of molten sheet metal. Only one gun turret at the front of the ship was still intact, like a flower standing in a pile of manure. The deck was at water level, with the hull almost entirely submerged.

As members of the *Shannon* crew boarded the ship, they expected to encounter carnage. In reality, the human toll was both terrible and unexpected; of the three hundred crew members, forty-two had died and one hundred were injured. The others were unharmed.

Robert Nichols was one of the miraculous survivors. Apart from taking some shrapnel to the back and hips, he had suffered no serious physical injuries. The blast from the first explosion had thrown him nearly the entire length of the deck. When he came to, he saw an officer carefully carrying ammunition to reload a gun that had run out. He was offering to help the man when another detonation shook the destroyer, causing him to drop the shell, which in turn exploded and blew the man to bits. Next, Nichols recalled seeing a gravely injured soldier lying on the deck. As he looked for help from the medical team, a third blast struck. Once the smoke cleared, the dying sailor was no more than a mangled pile of flesh.

Nichols was then assigned to the engine room where, until the attack was over, he pumped out water that threatened to sink the ship. One particular memory stuck with him: the sight of a lone brown boot he had spotted on the deck just after the first impact. The style left no doubt. It belonged to the kamikaze pilot. His foot was still inside.

The wreck of the USS *Aaron Ward* was towed to an American base near Kerama Retto, where it docked at dawn on May 4. The injured were administered medical care and those most gravely wounded were discharged, while the rest—like Nichols—were granted a furlough to return home. All crew members were immediately awarded a Purple Heart. The ship was deemed beyond repair and transported to the New York Yard, where it was to be sold for scrap.

While the destroyer was making its last voyage to Manhattan, the United States dropped atomic bombs on Hiroshima and Nagasaki on August 6 and 9, putting an end to the Pacific War and World War II. In less than four months, the naval Battle of Okinawa had claimed the lives of nine thousand American soldiers, most of them killed by the Japanese army's one thousand four hundred sixty-five kamikaze pilots. It was the deadliest naval battle in the Pacific theater.

Upon his return to New Albany, Robert Nichols was celebrated as a hero. In an interview with the *Courier Journal*, which sent a reporter to speak to Nichols as he stepped off the plane, the young man described the "fifty-two minutes of hell" he had just survived. "I will never quit wondering how I came through that experience," he said. "I can count six times that death stared me in the face. Each time I escaped was a miracle. When it was all over, all I thought about was home." He told them that as he rested on his bunk in the evenings, he had written letters to his mother, since he had no fiancée, and asked her to pray for him. He had held on thanks to her.

At the end of the interview, Nichols suggested that he would report for reassignment at the end of his furlough. He was lying. The nightmare of May 3 had changed him. If your country goes to war, then you have no choice but to fight for it, but war in itself is senseless—the way forward must first and foremost be through peace. That was his new philosophy. Now that World War II was over, serving in the army was out of the question. Shortly after the interview, in the privacy of his family home and with his mother as a witness, he burned his navy uniform in a coal bin.

The Nicholses' single-story home at 1823 Center Street was more a cottage than a house. New Albany was in a suburb bordering Louisville, the economic capital of Kentucky. Between the two cities ran the Ohio River, which also marked the border between Kentucky and Indiana. By the end of the war, the region was an industrial stronghold, with two Ford factories in addition to the famous bourbon distilleries.

Robert's mother, Alpha Nichols née Schreiber, was a seamstress at Mr. Fine & Sons, a men's shirt factory on East Main Street. His father, Silas Nichols, was a First World War veteran and worked as a skilled laborer at W. R. Martin Co., a machine shop in Louisville. Alpha was strict, with a stormy disposition, while Silas was submissive and reserved. They were married on May 9, 1914, and their first child, John, died in infancy. They later had three more boys: James, born in 1924; Robert, born in 1926; and Marvin, the youngest, born in 1929.

Called to serve in the military before finishing high school, Robert Nichols did not get his high school diploma. This meant that once back in civilian life, he was unable to apply for college. In Kentucky and throughout the country, Coca-Cola was recruiting truck drivers to deliver soda to bars and restaurants, so this became his first job. It wasn't particularly engaging, but he took this opportunity to scout out nightclubs and bars where he could perform.

Ever since he was a teen, Robert had played the upright bass. So when he'd returned from the war, he and three other musicians had formed a band. They played "hillbilly music," an energetic southern country style featuring fiddle and banjo, with traditional tunes like the iconic "Cotton Eye Joe." The band was a hit.

The best-paid gigs, and thus the most coveted ones, were square dance events, which provided simple dance moves set to all sorts of country music.

Robert Nichols and his band were playing at one such event when he spotted a pretty young girl with good technique on the dance floor. Seventeen-year-old Laverne Korte had a slim waist and supple movements, which she had honed as a high-level dancer and competitive basketball player at Louisville High School. Her long black hair and hazel eyes enhanced her graceful silhouette. She liked to dance single but not alone. Her father, Herman Korte, was a furniture maker who, on weekends, would supplement his income by donning the colorful garb of a dance caller—the person who calls out the dance steps over the microphone.

For Laverne and Robert, it was love at first sight. They were wed on January 9, 1946, less than six months after their eyes first met. On the day of the ceremony, the bride wore a long blue crepe dress with white rosebuds along the bodice.

Nineteen days earlier, nine hundred miles west of the wedding, an eight-year-old boy named Joseph Chandler had died on a Texas highway.

❖

As both a veteran and a young husband, Robert Nichols was on a priority track for public housing. The couple moved into a new build in New Albany that consisted of two-story houses shared by two households. After several miscarriages, Laverne gave birth to Phil in 1947, then Charles in 1949. In 1952, the family moved to a three-bedroom apartment in the same building, which would allow them to make space for little David in two years.

Around the same time, Nichols applied for a job at General Electric. The American titan had just opened a massive one-thousand-acre industrial site in Louisville to manufacture household appliances. Although Nichols had no diploma, he did have a hidden talent: He was an excellent draftsman. He had taken technical drawing classes in high school, and he liked to sketch airplanes in his spare time. At General Electric, he was granted an opportunity when he landed a position at the lowest rung of the industrial design department.

The Nichols crew was more household than family. Like his father, Robert was excessively self-effacing, a ghost living under his own roof. He barely spoke to his wife, much less to his children, demonstrating neither anger nor joy. In the evenings and on weekends, he would read the newspaper in his armchair or just sit there doing nothing.

The only thing that seemed to bring him joy was spending time in the garage, chipping away at a personal project he'd begun before the war. He was building a rather peculiar mechanical device: a homemade machine gun. It was a little engineering marvel, assembled without instructions and made from pieces of wood and salvaged metal parts. Once completed, the fake but realistic weapon could even shoot plastic pellets.

Laverne was hardly warmer than her husband. Her father, a devout German Catholic immigrant, had passed on the virtues of hard work and austerity to his daughter. With her only brother, Laverne had grown up on a secluded farm in Indiana, twenty-five miles north of Louisville, where fun was considered a futile distraction. In addition to working as a furniture maker and dance caller, Herman tended to his fields. The Kortes were not poor, but they lived on very little. At Christmas, little Laverne would find a pair of socks beneath the tree, and for her birthday, three days later, there would be no party, no gifts. So, it's easy to understand why the Nichols family did not celebrate birthdays.

Just once, Laverne strayed from her upbringing and decided to bake a chocolate cake for her husband's twenty-eighth birthday. The birthday boy was in on the surprise. That evening, at the end of dinner, which was served in their cramped kitchen, as always, he exclaimed with uncharacteristic enthusiasm, "Time for cake!"

Phil, aged seven, and Charles, aged five, had not yet finished eating and sat quietly at the small square table. "Wait until the children are done," said Laverne. Her husband waited patiently until cake and candles were finally brought in. But before his wife could fetch a knife, Robert reached out, grabbed a handful of cake, and stuffed it into his mouth, looking satisfied. The rest of the family was speechless. Phil was old enough to have his own opinions, and this interaction left him thunderstruck. It was the first time he had seen his father express his own will about any aspect of their home life, and the result was disturbing, to say the least.

The incident contributed to his ill ease regarding his father. Phil didn't hate him; he just had no idea who this man was, this man he was forced to live with. Because Robert's wife encouraged him to show his kids some consideration, if not affection, he would sometimes take his two eldest sons to a baseball game. Once there, he would buy them pennants and hot dogs; even the worst of fathers couldn't skip that. He would rise for the national anthem, listen with a hand over his heart, then sit down and spend the rest of the game waiting for it to end. Never a pat on the back for his boys, not even a loving glance.

At least their mother would occasionally allow herself to hug or pat her children while still carrying on the tradition, long-standing in the Korte family, of corporal punishment with a leather strap that she kept on hand. If the Nichols children had waited to hear "I love you, son" before bed, they wouldn't have gotten much sleep.

In 1959, Robert brought home their first new car, a Ford station wagon, the classic family vehicle. Again, under pressure from his wife, he would sometimes load a tent into the roomy trunk and take the boys camping in nearby parks. He would set up camp, then let Phil and Charles horse around outside for the rest of the day.

In his work, Robert seemed a little more fulfilled. His talent set him apart from the rank-and-file draftsmen, which gave him access to the department's elite. In fact, his boss was so fond of him that he wanted to promote him to the rank of an engineer, which meant Robert would need a university degree, and General Electric agreed to fund his studies. In his new role, he often had to travel.

And Laverne, though she showed as little affection to her husband as her children, suddenly acted out in jealousy. She did not like knowing he was far away and in the company of God knew who. Her three pregnancies had cost her the slender build of her younger days, and she'd continued to gain weight since then. This made her irritable and suspicious. Robert was a kind of natural lightning rod and received her stormy outbursts impassively.

One evening in 1962, after dinner, the three boys—then aged fifteen, thirteen, and eight, respectively—were asked to gather around the kitchen table. Laverne and Robert were waiting for them, looking stern. Their two stools were set farther apart than usual.

"Well, tell them!" Laverne ordered her husband.

Robert stared at a speck of dust on the floor.

"Your mother and I are separating."

"It's not just a separation, it's a divorce!" Laverne corrected him.

Neither parent provided an explanation. They added that Phil and Charles would each have to decide which parent they wanted to live with, while little David would automatically stay with his mother. Robert would be packing his bags. And until Robert found a place to live, both spouses would live together under the same roof.

A few days later, Phil was driving through downtown Louisville on the passenger side of a friend's car when he noticed his father beside them at a red light. Robert Nichols was behind the wheel of a car that wasn't the family station wagon. He idled in the right lane, a little farther back, but it was him, no doubt about it. Beside him sat a redhead who looked to be in her twenties.

Robert didn't seem to notice his eldest son, who wanted to point out the coincidence and had rolled down his window to get his attention. "Dad!" The man's head did not move an inch. But the woman heard him. She glanced back and forth, from father to son, seeming both astonished and amused, as though she'd just figured out a good one. Then the light turned green, and both cars faded into the traffic.

When Phil returned home later that afternoon, his father was still out, but his mother was there.

"You will never guess who I saw on Preston Highway."

"Who?"

"Dad. And he was with a real pretty redhead."

Laverne went silent. Two days later, Robert packed his bags into the trunk of the Ford station wagon and moved out for good.

In the conflict between their parents, Phil and Charles quickly took sides. They would continue living with their mother. It wasn't the best option so much as it was the lesser of all evils. Although Laverne was far from being the perfect mother, Robert was barely a father at all. Nor had he expressed any desire to obtain custody of his children. Phil was relieved to be rid of this parent who was obviously indifferent to everything, including his sons. To feel abandoned, he would first have had to feel loved. This made Robert's subsequent attempt to win back his children all the more surreal.

One afternoon, Robert Nichols drove up to the house in a shiny red Ford convertible with white seats. Phil had just come home from school. To prepare for the divorce, Laverne had started a job as a hospital caregiver, and she was still at work. "That redhead really won this round," thought Phil, admiring his father's new car from the porch. He watched his father approach with what definitely counted as a smile by Robert Nichols's standards.

"Hey, do you want to come live with me? We'll move to another city, far from here. You'll see, we'll do plenty of fun stuff together."

We'll do plenty of fun stuff together.

Was this a joke? In over fifteen years, Robert Nichols had never expressed any interest in doing the slightest amount of "fun stuff" with any of his sons. He had to be forced into it, and when he gave in, he'd spend the entire day looking unbelievably grumpy.

Phil told his father to "go to hell" and slammed the front door.

Many years later, he would regret those words. But in that moment, they reflected a deep sense that this ersatz father couldn't care less about the world in general and about him in particular.

Shortly after this interaction, Robert moved 360 miles away to Dearborn, a suburb of Detroit on the western shore of Lake Erie. In Dearborn, he got an engineering job with a company that manufactured single-seat cars designed for the Indy 500, an annual race held at the Indianapolis Motor Speedway.

Phil figured he was done with this grim figure in his life, but his father resurfaced only a month after leaving. "Boys, your father wants the three of you to visit him," said Laverne. "You'll take a Greyhound bus there on your own. He's bought you tickets." The brothers weren't thrilled until they found out about the bus ride. They were about to hit the road on a cross-country adventure without any adult supervision. What a blast!

When they pulled into the Detroit bus station in the middle of the night, Robert greeted his children with his usual emotional sobriety. "He's going to show us his new home, his new life," thought Phil. Wrong. Their father made them get in the car, then drove away from the city lights, parked in front of some motel on the outskirts of town, dropped them off at a prepaid room, and took off. The three boys were left to themselves in the middle of nowhere—they couldn't believe it.

The next day, Robert picked up his sons at the reception area and took them to the Henry Ford Museum in Dearborn, which was the largest automotive museum in the world. Their father acted the same way he had throughout their childhood outings to the stadium and their camping trips, like a distant uncle tasked with chaperoning the boys. In the evening, he treated them all to a burger, then dropped his kids off at the motel, as he had done the day before.

On the second day, they took the Ford convertible across the Canadian border to spend a day at the Boblo Island Amusement Park. Every time the boys lined up to take a ride, their father stayed behind and sat on a bench, waiting for it to be over.

Back at the motel that evening, Phil started to feel that the joke was getting old. In New Albany, he had been dating a fifteen-year-old girl named Pam, with whom he'd been exploring his sexuality in the back seat of Laverne's Chevrolet. He missed his girlfriend, so he picked up the room phone, and they spent most of the night chatting. The next morning, when the boys met up with their father at the front desk, he was arguing with the motel clerk. He had been notified of an eight-dollar charge that would be added to his bill for phone calls made from the room. Robert was furious and immediately called the trip off, settled the bill, and left the boys at the bus station without saying a word.

They never saw him again.

Not a single member of the extended Nichols clan—his parents, his older brother James, his younger brother Marvin, or Laverne—would ever see him again.

Still, Robert Nichols's first life was not quite over yet. Though he had left, he continued to be involved in proceedings related to his divorce, which was granted by the Louisville court on March 19, 1964. He then wrote a letter to his parents, who still lived at 1823 Center Street in New Albany. Mailed from Dearborn, it was dated January 17, 1965. Robert thanked his mother for sending him old photos of Christmas Eves spent with his family, especially "the one of Phil that I forgot," and suddenly became nostalgic.

> *The pictures remind me how nice it was to be at home for Christmas. As the song says, "There's no place like home for the holidays."*

Two months later, on March 9, 1965, he wrote to his parents again. This time, it was a brief postcard.

> *Dear Mom and Dad,*
> *I am heading out west. All is well. Don't worry.*
> *Robert*

The postcard had been stamped by the post office in Stroud, Oklahoma, a town located halfway between Michigan and the Pacific Coast and a forty-five-minute drive from Tulsa, where young Joseph Chandler and his parents had once lived.

On March 20, 1965, Alpha and Silas Nichols received a third letter from their son. According to the postmark, it had been mailed from California, but for some reason, the return address on the envelope was a PO box in Dearborn. Over two pages, Robert shared that he was glad to have moved to the West Coast, saying, "I always wanted to live here," and told his parents he had found a job as a designer in an unnamed company. The pay was worse than in Detroit, but the contract would involve lots of travel, so he'd make up for it in expenses, he explained. Then he concluded:

> *Please do not worry about me. I am well and*
> *happy. I will write as often as I can and let you*
> *know how I am doing.*
> *Robert.*

He would not keep his word. This third letter was the last sign of life that the Nichols parents would ever get from their son.

Before dying for the first time and coming back to life under a different name, Robert Nichols sent one final piece of mail, from California, to a family member. It was delivered in the fall of 1965 to the Air Force training camp in Biloxi, Mississippi, where his eldest son was serving in the military. Phil found the mail in his locker and tore it open on the spot.

His address had been handwritten by his father—he was sure of this—but the envelope contained no letter, no signature, no writing. It wasn't empty though.

In the envelope, he found a penny.

Years later, when Phil Nichols came to realize his father was never coming back, he asked his mother which of the two spouses had initiated the divorce. It was Robert, she told him.

"And the only reason he gave me was '"One day, you'll know why."'"

Chapter 9

On June 20, 2018, journalist James Renner, a reporter for the alternative newspaper the *Cleveland Scene*, received an unpleasant phone call. In twenty-four hours, he was set to fly to Los Angeles to meet Colleen Fitzpatrick for an article about the rise of genetic genealogy. The DNA Doe Project she had just founded in April with Margaret Press had yet to resolve any cold cases, but the elusive Golden State Killer had recently been identified using techniques similar to those applied by the two women, techniques that had become a source of immense hope.

Fitzpatrick was on the line. She had bad news—she wouldn't be able to make their appointment, which had been planned months ago. She was all the more apologetic when she explained that the reason for the cancellation was confidential. Renner was furious but decided to make the trip anyway, as he had other meetings scheduled in the area.

A few minutes later, he got another call, this time from Peter Elliott. Elliott and Renner had known each other for a long time and had often worked on projects in which they had a shared interest. They were friendly.

"What are you doing tomorrow?" asked Elliott.

"I'm off to LA for work."

"You should stay in Cleveland."

"Why?"

"Take my advice."

Renner, unable to connect the dots, flew to California. But as soon as he landed in Los Angeles, his phone lit up with messages from colleagues who had reached out during the flight. "You're not at the press conference? They know who Chandler is!" Fitzpatrick had canceled because she was in Cleveland with US Marshal Peter Elliott to make a big announcement. This would have been nothing more than a minor inconvenience if Renner wasn't also missing the epilogue to a case that had become an obsession for him over the past twelve years due to its remarkably strange nature.

In fact, James Renner is the first to admit that his career is entirely based on his obsessive personality. That and an unfortunate story of love thwarted at first sight.

The moment eleven-year-old James saw Amy Mihaljevic's face—her chestnut eyes, her playful smile, her ponytail tied to one side like an orphaned pigtail—he realized what love was. To Renner, it was an injustice that she didn't go to the same school as him and wasn't in the same class. He would have spent the hours writing her little notes passed behind the teacher's back to woo her.

Renner lived in the southern suburbs of Cleveland, while Amy lived in the western suburbs. Well, at least that's where she had lived before being kidnapped. He had never actually crossed paths with her; Renner had fallen in love with Amy when he saw her school photo on the local news. The girl had just been abducted from a mall, where she'd gone on her own to buy a gift for her mother.

A composite drawing of the kidnapper was published, but the investigation was going nowhere. So Renner made it his mission to get the job done himself. On the way to and from school, Renner would scan the streets hoping to spot Amy's attacker in the crowd and then make him confess where he'd hidden the young boy's true love. In the evenings, he would sit glued to the

TV to find out the latest developments in the case and make note of any new clues collected by the police. His efforts were not enough. One hundred four days after Amy went missing, the local TV stations reported that her body had been found in a wheat field. She had been sexually assaulted and then strangled.

By 2003, Renner had become a journalist but had never forgotten that mischievous smile that captured his young heart. Since Amy's murderer was still at large, he decided to pick up his investigation where he had left off fifteen years prior. He interviewed witnesses, detectives, and family members; reviewed leads that had already been explored, including some that were shut down too soon; and opened new leads that he looked into himself.

The fact that professional ethics require some degree of detachment between reporters and their subjects made him quietly chuckle to himself; not only was this wishful thinking, but a journalist who reported facts without ever interfering was about as useful as a voice recorder. The press had a duty to serve the public, and when it came to legal matters, that meant trying to succeed where the police had failed.

Though he was unable to expose the murderer, Renner drew from these months of investigation to write a series of articles and then a book titled *Amy: My Search for Her*

Killer, published in 2006 and featuring the missing girl's school photo on the cover.

Publishing the story had two major consequences. It drove a new wave of tips and reports and triggered a period of acute paranoia for Renner. Waiting in line at the grocery store, he was convinced the guy in front of him had little girls tied up in his cellar. Antidepressants did nothing, which prompted him to book an appointment with a psychologist. The therapist submitted him to a personality test designed to detect possible psychotic disorders, the same test CIA recruits were required to take. She told him, "Your results are very close to those of serial killer Ted Bundy."

Renner was suffering from a kind of reverse Stockholm syndrome. He had spent so long chasing a deranged man that he had developed the psychopathic traits himself. To avoid sinking deeper into this headspace, and as counterintuitive as it may seem, the therapist recommended he keep writing about criminal cases. "It will help you channel that dark side," she explained.

Among the many news stories he perpetually lugged around in his mind was the peculiar case of Joseph Chandler. Renner had first read about it in 2003 in a *Plain Dealer* article about the challenges Tom Doyle encountered in attempting to solve the puzzle. He had immediately been fascinated by this image of an identity thief who died a hermit in a near empty studio apartment, leaving behind no fingerprints and no clues as to his past life. He figured it was probably the strangest mystery you could imagine.

Since then, the case seemed to have stalled, but the beauty of the enigma made it worth looking into. Plus, compared to tracking a child killer, investigating identity theft provided the added benefit of leaving his paranoid tendencies mostly undisturbed. Renner made his way to Eastlake, where he met with Chris Bowersock, the detective who had discovered Chandler's body; Mike Onderisin from Lubrizol; and others involved in the case.

He was the first to note an uncanny physical resemblance between Joseph Chandler and Stephen Campbell, a fugitive wanted by Wyoming marshals since 1982 for the attempted murder of his wife. Before the crime, Campbell was known to be a gifted and solitary electrical engineer and tinkerer. Renner published the results of his work in 2008 in a collection devoted to Cleveland's twelve greatest unsolved crimes.

When Peter Elliott took over the Chandler case in 2014, one of his first thoughts was to call Renner. Over time, as the two men developed a relationship built on trust, Renner became Elliott's official evidence launderer on Reddit. The social platform was a haven for web sleuths, amateur cyber investigators who take on major unsolved crimes and dissect them endlessly in the hopes of cracking the case. Most were freaks, but there were also a few sincere enthusiasts who were able to make use of the information or simply spread the word beyond traditional media channels.

Shortly after relaunching the investigation, Elliott invited Renner to his office. He had a surprise for him. Renner arrived to find all the sealed evidence spread across a large, round table: the revolver, the Seiko watch, the eyeglasses, the two guides to getting rich, a birth certificate in the name of the real Joseph Chandler, and even the white noise box that had been found in the safe. In the eyes of a man who possessed so little, these small things had likely been treasures. With the evidence laid before them, the peculiar story suddenly felt more real, almost alive. A bit sadder too. Whether these things belonged to a small-time identity thief or a dangerous fugitive, they were, above all, the possessions of an old hermit haunted by his strange whims.

Renner was allowed to photograph the evidence and post the shots in Reddit groups dedicated to cold cases, without mentioning his source, of course. Elliott

requested his services once more in 2016 when he asked
Renner to post about the story of Chandler's penile
injury, which had been treated in the hospital. In the
realm of sexual preferences, vacuum-assisted masturba-
tion was exotic enough to have made an impression on
the people who were direct or indirect witnesses, hence
Elliott's interest in sharing the story as widely as possible.

The Chandler case was an instant hit with web sleuths.
In the UnresolvedMysteries subreddit, which was one
hundred fifty thousand subscribers strong, it became a
favorite topic of debate. Speculation over the retiree's true
identity ranged from Jim Morrison to a former CIA spy
on the outs with the agency. Others thought that in the
story of the costume-themed birthday party, they had
found a brilliantly raised middle finger hiding the key
to this mystery. They speculated that Joe had used the
costume to show everyone his true colors by dressing up
as the mobster that he was.

According to one of the most popular hypotheses,
the man in the driver's license photo had similar features to an FBI sketch of a man named Dan Cooper.
On November 24, 1971, a man using that pseudonym
had boarded a Portland-Seattle flight. He was wearing
a black trench coat and carried a briefcase. Shortly after
takeoff, he told a flight attendant that the briefcase

contained a bomb and demanded that, upon landing in Seattle, they bring him $200,000 in a backpack as well as four parachutes. Without informing the passengers, the crew warned the company, which opted to comply.

On the tarmac, once the unsuspecting passengers had disembarked, the ransom and parachutes were handed over to the hijacker, who had remained on board. He then ordered the pilots to take off again and fly at a more moderate speed. Five minutes after takeoff, he jumped out of an emergency exit, taking his loot with him. The man was never found or identified. Aside from a physical resemblance that was debatable but not crazy, the fake Joseph Chandler and Dan Cooper were also about the same age in 1971. Both were highly intelligent and notoriously cold, and both had an innate sense of discretion.

At 1:00 P.M. on June 21, 2018, Elliott's press conference began in Cleveland, and a local TV station set up a live broadcast of the event over Facebook. It attracted thousands of online viewers who were eager to find out how the story ended. Standing by Elliott and genealogist Colleen Fitzpatrick were the Eastlake chief of police, the mayor of Eastlake, former lieutenant Tom Doyle,

and a surprise guest whom none of the many journalists in attendance recognized. When his name was called, the elderly man walked up to the lectern with a slight stoop. Despite his age, people watching the conference could see the family resemblance between this man and the photos of a young Robert Nichols displayed on the whiteboard beside him.

It was Phil, the eldest of the three Nichols siblings. He was now seventy years old and wore the same prominent glasses as his father. His light blue polo shirt and jeans contrasted with the formal outfits of the officials at the front of the room. He spoke slowly, in a typical Midwestern blue-collar accent. "Someone asked me earlier what my state of mind was. I don't feel any kind of animosity toward my father. I always hoped that he had found a happy life somewhere," he said wearily.

When his DNA was compared with a sample from the unnamed retiree, the last piece of the puzzle fell into place. Using a family tree provided by Fitzpatrick and Press, Elliott found Phil Nichols's address in online civil status records. He was living in Cincinnati, in southern Ohio, just a three-hour drive from Cleveland. When Elliott and his deputy showed up at Phil's door, they held off on explaining why they were there. They first asked him about his past, his childhood, and his parents. When stories about this vanishing father came up, they asked to see photos.

Phil had three undated shots: a high school photo, a snapshot of Nichols in a suit and tie, and a photograph taken on the sidewalk in front of the family home. In the last shot, Robert Nichols is wearing a short-sleeved shirt and smiling with, in his right hand, a revolver pointed at the camera. At this point, the marshals were sure they were in the right place and explained the reason for their visit.

When he learned the truth about his father's final years, Phil Nichols felt a kind of relief, the feeling experienced by someone who has pretended to give up, to stop feeding all hope, without really managing to let go entirely. He agreed to provide a saliva sample for DNA comparison. The procedure was merely a formality. From the moment he saw Phil Nichols's face in the doorway, Elliott knew he had just solved a sixteen-year-old mystery.

Well, at least one part of the mystery.

They'd broken through one wall, but the Eastlake John Doe was a double-walled enigma.

They had found out *who* was hiding behind Joseph Chandler, but that didn't explain *what* he was hiding.

❖

Instinctively, Elliott was always convinced that the mystery retiree was a big-league fugitive. James Renner thought so too, and that's why both men were so dedicated to this strange case. When they found out who Chandler really was, it deepened their shared conviction and seemed to magnify it. Nothing in Robert Nichols's known past explained the stolen identity or the lengths to which he had gone to remain hidden. When they compared descriptions of the young New Albany father and his Eastlake alter ego, Elliott and Renner came to the same conclusion: The enemy Robert Nichols had so desperately tried to escape was neither marriage, nor fatherhood, nor the weight of social convention, nor the ghosts of war.

He was buying time.

In most of the United States, the statute of limitations applies to all offenses but violent crimes.

Between his disappearance in 1965 and his reappearance in 1978 under a name that was not his own, Nichols must have led a third life. The life of a murderer who had gone unpunished.

And for both men, a cluster of persistent clues traced the outline of a figure so spectacular that the theory had previously been dismissed as outlandish.

They were looking at the legendary Zodiac Killer.

Chapter 10

The Zodiac is to the United States what Jack the Ripper is to England—a faceless serial killer who, though once the subject of criminal news coverage, has long since become a figure of pop culture.

Fifty-four books, thirty-nine fiction and documentary films, and thousands of articles have been published about this incredible enigma. More than fifty years later, every minute break in the case or supposedly new lead has caused a media frenzy to ripple across the planet. Some believe the very concept of a serial killer, in an academic sense, began with this case; unlike mass murderers, the Zodiac did not choose his victims randomly but followed a logic of his own, a criminal pattern that repeated itself, accumulating corpses like an artist building his body of work.

On August 1, 1969, the investigation into the Zodiac murders was triggered not by a body discovery but by a series of four handwritten letters. Three were addressed to a few news outlets in San Francisco, and the fourth was sent to the police. In an arrogant tone, the author claimed responsibility for the shooting deaths of three students in the area just a few weeks earlier. Three teens, two female and one male, had been shot in their vehicles.

Along with his confession, he provided a sequence of four hundred eight cryptic pictograms, a code that he said would reveal his identity once deciphered. Six days later, a fifth letter was sent to the press, adding details about the three crimes that only the killer could have known. It began with five words that have become the stuff of lore—"This is the Zodiac speaking"—and ended with a symbol, a circle with a cross over it that looked like a target.

More letters came in, following more murders. Each letter was accompanied by a new cryptogram to be deciphered. In his twentieth missive, sent to the *San Francisco Chronicle* on January 29, 1974, the Zodiac took stock of his criminal odyssey: he claimed thirty-seven victims. Officially, the San Francisco police attributed only seven victims to the Zodiac Killer: five dead, two wounded, all students. These crimes were perpetrated between December 1968 and October 1969, all within seventy miles of San Francisco Bay. Despite a mammoth investigation involving two thousand five hundred suspects and even the CIA, they remain unpunished to this day.

In the Chandler investigation, the Zodiac Killer first appeared on May 2, 2005, in a letter addressed to Lieutenant Tom Doyle of the Eastlake police. The sender was Mia Marcum, the head of the Ohio Doe Network, an NGO that gives names back to the anonymous dead by linking them to missing persons cases. Her letter highlighted physical similarities between the fake Chandler and the Zodiac Killer, as described by his surviving victims: identical height, about five feet eight, and brown hair. Slight build.

In a strange coincidence, one week later, the police station received a fax from someone following the same hunch. The sender, a man from New Jersey who was obsessed with the Zodiac case, had come across the story of the unnamed retiree. He figured he'd try entering the fake Chandler's name in the government's online database of deceased social security beneficiaries. Results showed a Joseph Chandler, born in 1950 and deceased in 1994, whose last known address had been in San Rafael, in the San Francisco Bay Area. The New Jersey

sleuth acknowledged that the dates of birth and death
were not a match for the Eastlake John Doe and that
perhaps both men had simply shared the same name.
Besides, even if it was him, the fact that he'd lived in the
Bay Area in 1994 didn't mean he'd massacred innocent
people twenty-five years earlier.

None of it was all that serious.

What made this hypothesis much less laughable in 2018
was a series of disturbing coincidences between the two
mysteries that came up while reconstructing Robert
Nichols's life.

    1. The Napa postmark:

      The Zodiac Killer left behind four crime
scenes spread out over a swath of Northern
California. Of the seven victims attributed
to him by the authorities, two were stabbed
seventy miles north of San Francisco, on the
shores of Lake Berryessa, in Napa County.

      When Phil Nichols, Robert Nichols's
eldest son, told Elliott the story of the
envelope containing a penny he'd received

from his father, the marshal asked to see it. Phil apologized—he had gotten rid of this painful reminder. But one detail had stuck with him: He remembered that the post-mark was from the Napa post office, which was a half-hour drive from Lake Berryessa, where Robert Nichols had thus likely been living. The letter had been sent in the fall of 1965, only four years before the Zodiac killings began.

2. The Richmond letter:

Robert Nichols's last letter to his parents, dated March 20, 1965, had been stamped by the post office in Richmond, a midsized town in the San Francisco Bay Area. While the Zodiac claimed no victims in that area, the town was centrally located, halfway between Vallejo and San Francisco's Presidio Heights neighborhood, where two of the four crimes had occurred. The murders were committed in 1969, and in a letter sent that same year, Nichols wrote "I like living here" and said he'd found a good job, two clues suggesting that he hoped to stick around.

3. The Cheri Jo Bates case:

A year after his divorce, Robert Nichols wrote to the Louisville Family Court to obtain a copy of the judgment, which he claimed he had never received. Elliott managed to recover the letter, dated July 4, 1965, which featured a return address in Nichols's name, in Los Angeles's upscale Brentwood neighborhood.

On October 30, 1966, eighteen-year-old Cheri Jo Bates was stabbed to death on a college campus in Riverside, a city in the Greater Los Angeles area. Some investigators believe this was the Zodiac's first murder. The victim was a student, and the killer claimed responsibility for his crime in two anonymous letters sent to a Riverside newspaper and the local police. A month later, a macabre poem was found etched into a desk in the campus library and was automatically attributed to the murderer. It was signed with two initials: an *r* as in Robert, followed by a badly drawn letter *n* as in Nichols, or an *h*, depending on the interpretation.

4. The handwriting:

Like the Zodiac in his ciphers, Nichols
wrote exclusively in block capitals. There
are significant commonalities in both their
handwriting samples, with uncommon
quirks like the need to fill gaps by placing
commas between two words that are too
spaced out or a tendency to misspell fairly
common terms despite a relatively elevated
writing style. For instance, the killer wrote
"buton" instead of "button," while Nichols
wrote "thaught" instead of "thought."

Some more tenuous analogies were also added to the
list. Experts have suggested that the Zodiac Killer spent
some time in the navy because a boot print found at
one of the crime scenes matched a type of boot popular
among those serving in the navy. One FBI profiler por-
trayed the Californian psychopath as lonely, supremely
intelligent, and prone to a form of social paranoia—all
attributes that Nichols shared.

And then there are the facts that don't fit.

If Nichols was the Zodiac Killer, with the entire
nation's police force looking for him since 1969, why

wait until 1978 to change his identity? Barring a significant stretch of the imagination, and despite the fact that both men wore glasses, Nichols looks nothing like the composite drawing published by the San Francisco police. As for the murder of Cheri Jo Bates, the Riverside police do not believe it to be the work of the Zodiac Killer, though they have not been able to formally rule it out.

Thesis, antithesis. When the time came for a synthesis, Elliott considered that a reasonable person might see Robert Nichols and the Zodiac Killer as one and the same.

Shortly before Nichols's identity was made public, Elliott discussed his theory over the phone with the San Francisco and Napa police. His California colleagues welcomed the hypothesis with measured enthusiasm, agreeing to share only select aspects of the case. When Elliott raised the possibility of providing Nichols's DNA so it could be compared with that of the Zodiac Killer, they explained their lack of enthusiasm. The police assigned to this case admitted that the genetic profile they had was taken from a postal stamp found on a letter sent by the serial killer. Not only was the sample highly incomplete, but no one could say for certain that it belonged to the killer. Evidence-handling protocols did not exist in the late 1960s, so any police officer or other person involved in the case could have touched it. Still, a DNA comparison was carried out, and although the result was negative, it did not disqualify Elliott's theory.

The Zodiac theory was neither good nor bad. As it was, it had simply led to a dead end.

Throughout the press conference to announce Robert Nichols's identity and known past, Peter Elliott displayed three yellowed photos that Phil Nichols had provided. At the end of the event, he made a solemn plea, asking witnesses to come forward. Between 1965 and 1978, in California, or in the suburbs of Detroit, or in South Dakota, or elsewhere in the country, this strange man must have caught the attention of some colleague, business owner, or neighbor with his unwillingness to speak, his bizarre tics, and twisted stories. Even the most insignificant memory could help pin him to a specific place at a specific time, which would provide a new opportunity to tie him to an unsolved crime. "Robert Ivan Nichols never wanted to be found throughout his lifetime, even into his death. And someone out there may hold the key as to why," he said.

In addition to the US Marshals' motto, Elliott had his own personal motto. When a case was so hard to crack that he got discouraged, it would remind him of the noble purpose behind his work: "There's always more victims than the victim." Family, friends, colleagues. The people who, like Robert Nichols on May 3, 1945, were knocked over by the blast of an explosion. We pay tribute to the dead, but we need to seek justice for the living.

In 2023, five years after Elliott's unanswered call for witnesses, his department is still investigating the case, driven by his hunch that someone out there, like him, is hoping to uncover the truth.

The Sticker

There is a well-documented history of economic decline in Midwestern cities as a result of offshoring. Detroit was the hardest hit, then Chicago, Pittsburgh. . . . Dozens of economists and sociologists came to their bedsides to analyze their long road to resilience and publish countless studies. Only Cleveland was left out of this list. The fate of Ohio's former industrial marvel generated such utter indifference that no public expert deemed it worth taking a closer look.

Though this odd truth may not solve the last mysteries of the Chandler case, perhaps it can shed light on the story's greater context. This is more than just the tale of one person's stolen identity; it is, above all, the story of a large-scale disappearance. About an economic Eden that vanished in the tumult of globalization. About an average American city that was downgraded but not entirely erased from academic and media radars. About a time before social media and digital tracking when you could flee the ghosts of your past with a real chance of outrunning them. About a husband and father, Robert Nichols, who knew he could lead his second life here as he saw fit: silent, hiding in the world's shadow.

In the 1980s, as "The Cleve" struggled to move on from the steel industry, the city turned toward the service sector, forcing its economy into banking, insurance, and health care. The shift was mirrored in the changing architecture. The once tallest building in Cleveland, the Terminal Tower—an Art Deco skyscraper symbolizing the industrial golden age—lost its title to a skyscraper built by the regional Key Bank. The national press, which had long enjoyed calling Cleveland a "mistake by the lake," now gave it the more flattering moniker "Comeback City."

Bolstered by this renaissance, Cleveland aspired to become a tourist destination. In 1994, the town celebrated the inauguration of a huge sports complex including an ultramodern stadium, while the Rock & Roll Hall of Fame Museum opened the following year. Cleveland could now boast that it had been the first city with a dedicated rock and roll radio station. Both projects also aimed to bring life back into the downtown core, which had become deserted after years of exodus and rampant crime.

By the early 2000s, though Cleveland may not have regained its former glory, it had become a prosperous midsized city. But nobody could have anticipated that it would one day be "cool." When LeBron James signed on with the Cavaliers, he ended a fifty-two-year losing streak in which none of Cleveland's three teams—football, basketball, baseball—had won a national title. This quiet city, once mocked, suddenly embodied the fantasy of exhausted city dwellers looking to escape the urban bustle without wasting away in a trailer in the backwoods of Kentucky. It became a place for weekend getaways, where you could have an ice cream by Lake Erie, see a concert by the world-renowned municipal orchestra, or enjoy a play in one of Cleveland's ten theaters in Playhouse Square, the best-equipped neighborhood in the United States, after Broadway.

In 2010, the city that once seemed to be the armpit of the Midwest landed its own sitcom, *Hot in Cleveland*, in which three cynical Californian forty-somethings accidentally end up in Cleveland, where they rediscover simple pleasures. A *30 Rock* episode, set in Cleveland

and aired in 2016, later cemented this stereotype. One of the lines even gave rise to the popular saying "Let's go to Cleveland," a kind of call to leave crowded urban chaos for quieter, greener spaces.

Eastlake did end up making it into the history books too, though, predictably, in the strangest of ways. On August 14, 2003, in the middle of the afternoon, the northeastern United States was hit by a massive blackout. Fifty-five million Americans were left in the dark for seven hours or more. The one hundred deaths and $6 billion in damages were nothing compared to the trauma of a country that thought it was safe from such a disaster.

Because North America's power grid is largely inter-connected, it took federal investigators eight months to identify patient zero in this chain reaction: a little coal-fired power station in Eastlake. Some overgrown trees had fallen onto a high-voltage transmission line, causing a short circuit and subsequent domino effect.

Tom Doyle occasionally picked up shifts as a secu-rity guard at the plant and was there that day. He was sitting in the guardhouse when he heard a huge *Bang!* then saw the director of the power plant headed his way, screaming, "What happened?" Tom shot back, "If you're the one asking the question, we are in deep shit."

The Eastlake coal-fired power station was one of the first victims of President Barack Obama's climate commitments. At the time of its closure in 2012, it still employed three hundred fifty people. The shutdown sparked anger among locals, who decried this considerable economic blow. Deprived of coal taxes, the municipality managed to avoid bankruptcy by implementing a sharp increase in local taxes and making drastic cuts to public services—the number of police officers dropped from forty to twenty.

During the 2016 presidential race, Donald Trump made reviving the coal industry his main campaign promise in the Midwest. In Eastlake, as in the rest of Ohio, he won by a landslide. But he never reopened the plant, and the huge chimney, now empty, still dominates the landscape.

With the exception of Detective Chris Bowersock, who moved to Arizona to escape the schizophrenic northern Ohio weather—according to a local proverb, it can snow in August—all people involved in the Chandler case still live in the area, now twenty years after the body was found. "The FBI guys who came to work with us loved coming here," says Tom Doyle. "They said Cleveland was America's best kept secret."

When his old friend Peter Elliott called to say he'd found a DNA sample for the Eastlake John Doe by contacting county hospitals, Doyle blamed himself for not having thought of that. Since then, he's been trying to make up for it. Doyle, a history buff, found a book on Amazon that retraced the USS *Aaron Ward*'s dramatic final hours. Based on officers' logs and interviews with survivors, *Brave Ship, Brave Men* describes, minute by minute, the ship's twenty-four hours in hell. The author pays tribute to all crew members, and their names are listed in the appendix. Astonishingly, Robert Nichols's name is missing and does not appear anywhere in the story.

Did he lie about his heroic past? Did he disappear and change his identity out of fear of having to explain himself one day? When Doyle noticed the omission, he was beside himself and immediately called Elliott to share his discovery. But the lead was no good. Elliott explained that he'd confirmed Nichols was in fact on the destroyer, and his military records proved it. True to his reputation as a relentless bulldog, Doyle has conducted a parallel investigation to verify a second hypothesis: If Nichols was on board, perhaps an incident involving him had been kept secret and could explain his crazy decision.

Tom Doyle is not the only one to think the Eastlake retiree was running away from something other than a crime. Phil Nichols would like to believe that the key to the puzzle is nothing spectacular; his father probably wanted to avoid paying child support—plain and simple. After all, Robert Nichols was pathologically stingy. From clothes and outings to school supplies, he never spent a penny on his children. His share of the expenses was covered by his parents and grandparents.

This same proclivity was also behind his dogged attempts to have Phil transferred from a Catholic private school, in which Laverne had enrolled him, to a public school. And it was an unpaid bill that had brought the weekend in Detroit to an abrupt end. "They're getting closer." Joseph Chandler had whispered this to his colleagues at Lubrizol before vanishing. What if, instead of the FBI, "they" was referring to bailiffs he thought might turn up on his doorstep?

As for James Renner, he still believes the Zodiac theory is the most convincing lead. Yet when he began investigating the case, he first looked for answers in his imagination. The Chandler mystery inspired his first novel, *The Man from Primrose Lane*, published in 2012. It is the story of David Neff, a successful true crime writer who has to grapple with the unsolved murder of a quiet hermit in Akron, Ohio. The locals called him "the man from Primrose Lane," and he'd walk around the neighborhood, rain or shine, always wearing a pair of mittens.

When the reporter manages to enter his house, where no fingerprints are left behind, he is struck by how bare the space is. The drawers are empty, there are only two shirts in the laundry room, and a few books sit on a shelf, including *Guitar for Dummies* and *Surviving the Apocalypse for Dummies*. The novel begins like a detective story and eventually shifts into science fiction in the last third. It turns out the man from Primrose Lane was a time traveler from the future who had come to prevent his wife's suicide—David Neff's wife. The old man with the mittens was him in thirty years.

The book was a minor success and was picked up by Hollywood. Initially, Warner Bros. sought to make a film adaptation starring Bradley Cooper, but it was eventually shut down. As of 2023, a TV series was in development, directed by Alexandre Aja, the son of Alexandre Arcady, a French director with an established career in the US. When the novel was translated into French, the publisher opted for the title *L'obsession*, which translates to "the obsession" in English, without realizing that it applied to David Neff's quest just as much as it did to the author's relationship with the story.

In online sleuthing communities, the Chandler case has lost its appeal. Once his identity was made public, enthusiasm plummeted among sleuths on Reddit. The photos of his belongings posted by James Renner at Peter Elliott's request are still online.

Elliott was especially hoping one particular piece of evidence would make new witnesses come forward and still believes it might help them to finally solve the case: a sticker from the *Peanuts* comic strip. Carefully preserved in Nichols's little safe in the Dover Place Apartments, the sticker features one of the comic's characters, a small yellow bird named Woodstock. He's Snoopy's best friend and is also the only character who never speaks. Or rather, he speaks in an unknown language that only Snoopy can understand.

On the sticker, the bird is smiling, feet slightly off
the ground and wings outstretched as if he were about
to take flight. Above are three words: "Way to go!"
According to the copyright symbol at the bottom of
the sticker, it was made in 1965. When the sticker was
pulled from the safe, it was in mint condition, further
proof that it had significant sentimental value to Nichols.
There must have been a reason.

Mike Onderisin, the supportive Lubrizol colleague who
became a key source of information for investigators,
died in 2020. He succumbed to cancer at the age of
seventy-nine, surrounded by loved ones, at his home in
Painesville. In his last years, he refused to speak with
journalists who came to his door. He was overwhelmed
by the scale of media and legal attention the story had
attracted. He was survived by his wife, Marilyn, who
shared a Thanksgiving dinner and her fiftieth birthday
party with Robert Nichols. As a matter of principle, she
declined all requests for interviews. She believes that if
her husband's colleague wanted to be buried with his
secret, then that wish should be honored. In her private
conversations, she still calls him "Joe."

As for Robert Nichols's ex-wife Laverne Korte, she once again took up her maiden name and, in July 1965, married a man she met at a dance class. John McBride was a postal worker and World War II veteran. Upon his return from the war, McBride had become a hopeless alcoholic, drinking pint after pint of beer for breakfast. He could be violent when he was drunk.

In turn, to cope with her toxic home life, Laverne became addicted to sedatives that she stole from her job at the hospital. One day, the couple decided to kick their respective addictions and get clean together through faith. They became pillars of the community in their local parish and lived sober and happy for the rest of their lives.

"One day, you'll know why," Robert explained when he left Laverne.

She died in 1992, at the age of sixty-two, without ever finding out why.

❖

The first of her three sons to join her was David. He was the youngest Nichols sibling and died in 2015 of a devastating sinus cancer at the age of sixty-one. He was only eleven when his father left home. He worked half his life at Philip Morris as a maintenance person before resigning to become a truck driver. David was married to the same woman until his death and had four children. Of the three Nichols brothers, he was likely least affected by the curious fate his father chose for himself.

Charles, the middle child, spent his old age in the green, rolling countryside of Northeast Georgia. As a younger man, he married his high school sweetheart and then moved to Atlanta to work at the Delta Air Lines head-quarters. Though he was initially hired as a maintenance technician, he worked his way into upper management. Charles was a father of four and an introverted man who never opened up about his essentially absent father.

When Phil considered transferring their father's urn from the Painesville cemetery to the family's home-town, New Albany, he finally learned what had been on Charlie's mind for so many years. "I don't want to spend a dime on him, he can stay right where he is," he said categorically.

At age seventy-three, Charles now lives in a nursing home. He suffers from advanced Parkinson's disease.

His father's ashes are still stored in the Painesville cemetery columbarium, behind a plaque engraved with a name that is not his.

Unlike his youngest brother, Phil wasn't able to shed the stigma of his family's shadowy past. Whiskey by the gallon, cocaine, LSD, life on the street, prison, broken marriages . . . fifty shades of the same suffering all ate away at his life. He was fifteen years old when he made his first of three suicide attempts. His parents had just announced their separation. One evening, he went to the local drugstore, bought a pack of razor blades, and slit his wrists as soon as he stepped outside. Police officers on patrol called for help, and Phil was taken to a private, long-term psychiatric facility.

His father came around on the second day. He was no longer living in their family home but had not yet moved to Michigan and was staying somewhere in town. In response to his son's desperate act, his only reaction was something like "You seem to be doing fine," and with that, he immediately checked his son out of the hospital. A stay in a private facility would be pricey.

For Phil, the bottle was comforting, always there when he needed it, serving as a substitute father. More damaging than his other vices, Phil's alcoholism cost him his first marriage at the age of nineteen and the following two, as well as the family life he would have wanted for his three children. He worked in a printing plant, then as a truck driver, and eventually as a foreman in a metalworking shop.

After his second divorce, at the age of forty, he signed up to attend local Alcoholics Anonymous meetings and went through his first round of rehab. But he was soon sent to prison for nine months, over $30 of unpaid child support. When he got out, he fell back off the wagon, then got clean, relapsed, and so on. He has been sober since age fifty-three, when he moved into a sober-living home for recovering alcoholics in Cincinnati. Today, he is seventy-five and still lives there.

When asked how he was doing, he answered with a courteous smile. "I'm still alive. Barely, but I'm still alive."

Every crime leaves behind more victims than the victim.

Sometimes, secrets do too.

APPENDICES

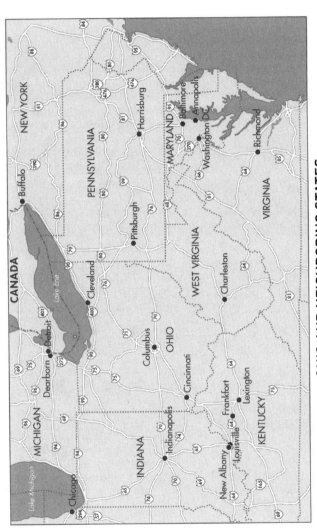

OHIO AND NEIGHBORING STATES

LAKE COUNTY

Timeline

1926—September 12: Robert Ivan Nichols is born in New Albany, Indiana.

1937—March 11: Joseph Newton Chandler III is born in Buffalo, New York.

1945—May 3: Destroyer USS *Aaron Ward* suffers a series of deadly kamikaze attacks off Okinawa. Wounded volunteer soldier Robert Nichols is awarded a Purple Heart.

1945—December 21: Eight-year-old Joseph Newton Chandler III and his parents die in a car accident in Weatherford, Texas.

1946—January 9: Robert Nichols and Laverne Korte are wed in Charlestown, Indiana. The couple settle down in New Albany and have three children: Phil, Charles, and David. Robert gets a job as an industrial designer at General Electric.

1964—March 19: The Nichols spouses get a divorce. Laverne retains custody of the three children, and Robert moves to Dearborn, Michigan.

1965—January 17: The first letter from Robert Nichols to his parents is mailed from Dearborn.

1965—March 9: Robert Nichols sends his parents a postcard mailed from Stroud, Oklahoma, near the Chandler family hometown. He announces his move to California.

1965—March 20: Robert Nichols's final letter to his parents is mailed from Richmond, a suburb of San Francisco.

1965—Fall: Phil Nichols receives mail from his father: an envelope containing one penny, sent from Napa, north of San Francisco. For Robert Nichols's loved ones, this will be the last sign of life they receive.

Between December 1968 and October 1969: In what will later become a criminal odyssey for the San Francisco area, an unknown gunman shoots five students and injures two more. Known as the Zodiac Killer, he has never been identified.

1978—September 25: Robert Nichols applies for and receives a social security card on behalf of Joseph Newton Chandler III in Rapid City, South Dakota.

1978—October 22: Robert Nichols, now Joseph Chandler, reappears in Eastlake, a suburb of Cleveland, Ohio, where he lives in a studio apartment. He works as an electrical engineer for the chemical giant Lubrizol.

1989—February 4: Joseph Chandler is hospitalized for lacerations on his penis.

1992—Spring: Joseph Chandler is invited to a birthday party and attends dressed as a mobster. He allows photographs to be taken of him.

1997: Joseph Chandler retires.

2000—March 5: Joseph Chandler undergoes a surgical operation to remove colon cancer.

2022—April 3: Joseph Chandler purchases a .38-caliber revolver at a local gun shop for $263.55.

2002—July 24: Probable date of Joseph Chandler's suicide in his Eastlake home. Cause of death: a .38-caliber bullet fired into the mouth.

2002—July 30: The decomposing body is found by Eastlake police. An investigation is launched to determine the cause of death.

2002—September 13: Mike Onderisin, a Lubrizol colleague, applies to become the administrator of Joseph Chandler's estate. His request is granted by the county's probate court, which opens a search for heirs.

2002—November 7: The Eastlake police department rules the death a suicide and closes the investigation into the cause of Joseph Chandler's death.

2003—April 28: In a report submitted to the probate court, private investigator Larry Morrow reveals that Joseph Chandler was living under a stolen identity. The Eastlake police reopen the investigation.

2008—January 15: The probate court closes all proceedings in the search for heirs, without further action.

2014—April 8: The Eastlake police suspend investigations into Joseph Chandler's true identity and hand over the case to Peter Elliott, chief marshal of the northern Ohio district.

2016—September: Peter Elliott enlists genealogist Colleen Fitzpatrick to solve the mystery and find Chandler's real name through genetic genealogy techniques.

2018—June 21: Peter Elliott and Colleen Fitzpatrick hold a press conference in Cleveland to announce that Joseph Chandler was actually Robert Nichols, a Pacific War veteran from Indiana. On the same day, the Eastlake police finally close the investigation, which began on July 30, 2002. The US Marshals' investigation stays open in the hope of finding the reasons that led Nichols to change his identity.

Nichols Family Tree

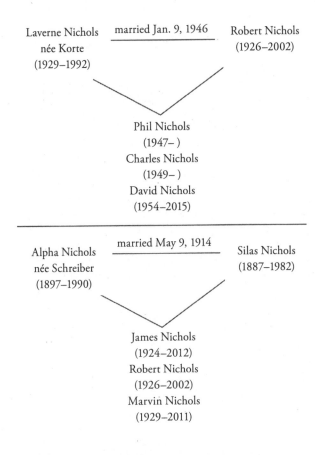

Laverne Nichols
née Korte
(1929–1992)

married Jan. 9, 1946

Robert Nichols
(1926–2002)

Phil Nichols
(1947–)
Charles Nichols
(1949–)
David Nichols
(1954–2015)

Alpha Nichols
née Schreiber
(1897–1990)

married May 9, 1914

Silas Nichols
(1887–1982)

James Nichols
(1924–2012)
Robert Nichols
(1926–2002)
Marvin Nichols
(1929–2011)

Sources

To date, no other book has been written on the Joseph
  Chandler enigma. No documentary or fiction films have
  tackled the story either.
In James Renner's *The Serial Killer's Apprentice: And
  12 Other True Stories of Cleveland's Most Intriguing
  Unsolved Crimes* (Gray & Company, 2018), one chapter
  is devoted to the case, and I heavily relied on it in my
  early investigation.
The recounting of the attack on the USS *Aaron Ward* is
  primarily based on Arnold Lott's book *Brave Ship,
  Brave Men* (revised edition, Naval Institute Press, 1994;
  Bobbs-Merrill, 1964, for the original edition).
Excerpts from Robert Nichols's interview with the *Courier
  Journal* upon his return from Okinawa come from the
  newspaper's archives.
One quote by Tom Doyle was taken from an article titled
  "Was dead imposter rocker or hijacker?" published by
  The Plain Dealer on June 5, 2003.
Other quotes and information in this book are from
  interviews and research conducted on the ground in
  September 2022 in Cleveland, Akron, Cincinnati,
  Eastlake County, and Ashtabula County, Ohio.

Acknowledgments

In addition to providing invaluable help, all my American contacts, without fail, showed me classic Midwestern hospitality and generosity. Thanking them is more than just a courtesy.

James Renner was especially helpful. Not only did he let me know that the Chandler case, which I had never heard of, was worthy of a book, but he also opened up many doors for me and shared access to his personal archives. I would like to take this opportunity to express my admiration for his career as a journalist and his work as a novelist.

Every reporter who lands in unknown territory needs a Larry Morrow and a Tom Doyle on their team. They were my guides, my fairy godmothers, my safecrackers, and in the end, they became my friends. For this book, I owe them so much, almost everything, in truth.

Phil Nichols agreed to reopen wounds suffered over the course of a difficult life, and he did so with extraordinary kindness and attention to detail. With his big heart, inner strength, and resilience, he is an exceptional man, and I am honored to have met him.

I am forever grateful to Peter Elliott and McKenzie Myers for granting me a significant amount of their precious time and even more so for the warm welcome they provided.

All my gratitude and more goes out to Chris Bowersock, Ted Kroczak, and Lou Formick. They were incredibly patient with my endless requests for clarification. They were always willing to share a good story, and if you had a laugh while reading this book, it was undoubtedly thanks to one of them.

Mike Lewis provided some precious tips as well as the coolest and most unlikely interview of my career, so a big thank you goes out to him.

Thanks to Jeffrey Offak for the beers and for keeping his cool when a stranger walked onto his property with his hands hidden in his jacket.

Thanks also to Kathleen Leskiw and Dave Franklin for the memories they shared with me, to Marah Morrison for her connections and advice, and to James O'Leary for being the best lawyer in my unsuccessful quest to secure an interview with his client.

Thanks again to Anne Burzynski for sowing the first seed that led to this book, and to Hubert Greiche for quickly rescuing a reporter who had gotten off to a bad start.

As always, thank you to my editors, Elsa Delachair and Stéphane Régy, for taking care of me.

Finally, thank you to Amandine, who compensated for my shortcomings as a busy young father, and to Doriane for forgiving this absence.

About the Author

Born in Paris, Thibault Raisse was a staff reporter at *Le Parisien* daily newspaper for nine years. He now works as a freelance journalist for French magazines *Society* and *Elle*, with a special interest in unsolved crime stories. He coauthored the best-selling true crime book *Xavier Dupont de Ligonnès: L'Enquête*, which was published in 2020.

CRIME INK PRESENTS

FRANCE'S LEADING TRUE CRIME JOURNALISTS INVESTIGATE AMERICA'S MOST NOTORIOUS CASES — ONE FOR EVERY STATE IN THE UNION.

Each title revisits an infamous crime, replete with all the hard facts and gruesome details, and brings fresh new perspectives to these storied cases. Taken together, the series reveals a dark national legacy, state-by-state, from sea to shining sea . . .

NEW YORK:
THE ALICE CRIMMINS CASE
ANAÏS RENEVIER
TRANSLATED BY LAURIE BENNETT
ISBN: 978-1-61316-629-1
The case that rocked New York City in the summer of '65. Two children disappear and turn up dead. Their beautiful and promiscuous mother is convicted in the court of public opinion . . . but did she commit the crime?

CALIFORNIA:
THE GOLDEN STATE KILLER CASE
WILLIAM THORP
TRANSLATED BY LYNN E. PALERMO
ISBN: 978-1-61316-631-4
For years a methodical killer stalked the shadows of sunny California. Responsible for at least fifty assaults and thirteen murders, an unlikely modern development led to an arrest more than forty years after his reign of terror began.

OHIO:
THE CLEVELAND JOHN DOE CASE
THIBAULT RAISSE
TRANSLATED BY LAURIE BENNETT
ISBN: 978-1-61316-633-8
A body is discovered by police in 2002 . . . but it doesn't match its name. The deceased had assumed a false identity. Who was he really? And what other secrets was he hiding?